TECHNOLOGY SUPPLEMENT *to accompany*

FINANCIAL MANAGEMENT

Theory and Practice

Eighth Edition

EUGENE F. BRIGHAM
UNIVERSITY OF FLORIDA

LOUIS C. GAPENSKI
UNIVERSITY OF FLORIDA

THE DRYDEN PRESS
HARCOURT BRACE COLLEGE PUBLISHERS

FORT WORTH PHILADELPHIA SAN DIEGO NEW YORK AUSTIN ORLANDO SAN ANTONIO
TORONTO MONTREAL LONDON SYDNEY TOKYO

Address for Editorial Correspondence
Harcourt Brace College Publishers, 301 Commerce Street, Suite 3700, Fort Worth, TX 76102

Address for Orders
Harcourt Brace & Company, 6277 Sea Harbor Drive, Orlando, FL 32887
1-800-782-4479

ISBN: 0-03-018687-0

Printed in the United States of America

8 9 0 1 2 3 4 5 6 023 9 8 7 6 5 4 3 2

The Dryden Press
Harcourt Brace College Publishers

PREFACE

This *Technology Supplement* is intended to provide students with the skills necessary to use the technological tools most commonly applied in financial analysis: namely, financial calculators and spreadsheets. Also, since presentation of results is an important part of the managerial process, we provide some information on presentation software. Of course, it is impossible to turn someone into a calculator or spreadsheet or presentation software expert with short tutorials, but an understanding of the tutorials in this supplement will enable students to perform all of the calculator analyses—such as time value of money and linear regression—discussed in the text. Furthermore, an understanding of the spreadsheet tutorial will provide students with the skills necessary to create, modify, and use the typical spreadsheet models that accompany cases, and an understanding of presentation software will help students convey their findings and recommendations.

The supplement is divided into two major parts: Part I, which contains several sections dealing with the most commonly used financial calculators; and Part II, which contains the spreadsheet tutorial. Users of The Dryden Press finance textbooks are authorized to have sections, or this entire supplement, copied and sold to students (at cost).

Dana Aberwald Clark, Brent Gibbs, Darryll Parker, and Dan Zinn helped create the tutorials, and Carol Stanton and Susan Purcell produced the final manuscript. We have tried to make the *Technology Supplement* as clear and error-free as possible; however, there are almost certainly some mistakes and unclear sections. Any suggestions for improving this supplement would be greatly appreciated.

Eugene F. Brigham
Louis C. Gapenski
Department of Finance
College of Business Administration
University of Florida
Gainesville, FL 32611-2017

September 1997

CONTENTS OF THE TECHNOLOGY SUPPLEMENT

Introduction to Financial Calculators

The history of the modern pocket calculator dates back to the creation of the abacus. The abacus, which was invented thousands of years ago, offered an easy way of adding and subtracting. Plus, it could also be used for multiplication and division. While this was a revolutionary innovation in its time, the evolution of calculating devices over the following centuries proved to be somewhat slow and methodical. As America moved through the industrial revolution, mechanical calculators became more sophisticated, but they were still very bulky and relatively limited in their computational capabilities. However, as with many other products, the evolution of calculating devices progressed dramatically as the world entered the age of electronics.

Since the invention of the integrated circuit in 1958, the power to incorporate more and more capabilities into a single chip of silicon has truly changed the world. At that time, the modern era of microelectronics was in its infancy. In 1967, engineers were still in the beginning stages of exploring the uses and advantages of metal-oxide semiconductor (MOS) integrated circuits, invented only nine years earlier by Texas Instruments. In 1967, a Texas Instruments team of engineers developed the first electronic handheld calculator. This marked the first time MOS integrated circuits were used in a product that had large commercial market potential.

Creating this miniature machine entailed more than just figuring out the logic and executing it as integrated circuits. The complexity, small size, and low power required by the calculator were unprecedented. Although the device was only capable of performing basic arithmetic functions (addition, subtraction, multiplication, and division), the handheld calculator was truly an amazing accomplishment for its time.

Initially, handheld calculators were very expensive relative to their limited calculating capabilities. Continued advances in computer technology, however, have dramatically improved the price/performance ratio. In fact, advanced calculations that 25 years ago would have required a room full of computing devices can now be quickly and easily performed with a handheld calculator that costs less than $40.00. All of the major calculator manufacturers produce calculators which can be used for basic arithmetic functions as well as for scientific, statistical, or financial calculations.

Financial calculators are designed to meet the special needs of professionals working in a finance function as well as finance students. Early financial calculators were distinguished from "regular" calculators by virtue of having built-in time value of money functions such as present value and future value of lump sums and annuities. Today, financial calculators run the gamut from only basic time value functions to relatively expensive calculators that allow users to program their own financial algorithms.

This tutorial, which focuses specifically on financial calculators, is intended to provide an overview of how to perform the most common types of finance problems. The models covered are the Texas Instruments BAII PLUS, the SHARP EL-733A, and the Hewlett-Packard HP-12C, HP-10B, and HP-17BII. This is by no means an exhaustive list of financial calculators, but these specific models were chosen for three reasons. First, all of the models selected are capable of performing advanced financial calculations including, but not limited to, time-value-of-money, cash flow analyses, and linear regression. Second, these calculators appear to be the most commonly sold and used on college campuses. Finally, all of these calculators can be purchased for under $100, so they are affordable to the average college student. In fact, the EL-733A, HP-10B, and HP-12C typically sell for under $40.00. Obviously, there is some trade-off between price and performance, but any of the calculators outlined in this tutorial are more than adequate for most college-level finance courses.

Hewlett-Packard 10B Tutorial

To begin, look at the face of the calculator. Every key (except one, the gold shift key) on the 10B has two functions: each key's primary function is noted in white on the key itself, while each key's secondary function is noted in gold above the key. To use the function on the key, simply press the key. To access the gold function above each key, first press the key with the solid gold face, which we will call the "gold shift" key, and then press the desired function key. (Note that the gold shift key is near the lower left corner of the calculator keyboard.)

Turning the Calculator On and Off

To turn on the calculator, press [C].

Note that the ON key is on the lower left corner of the keyboard—the face of the key has a white "C," while the word "ON" appears below the key. Also, we will designate keys throughout this tutorial by the use of small boxes, as above. To conserve the battery, the calculator turns itself off about 10 minutes after your last keystroke.

To turn the calculator off, press ■ [OFF].

Here we are using the solid black square to represent the gold shift key. Thus, the keystrokes to turn the calculator off are (1) press the gold shift key, and (2) then press the C key. Note that the word "OFF" appears above the C key in gold. Thus, by pressing the gold shift key first, we are activating the gold function above the C key, which is the off function. Also, note that pressing the gold shift key places a little "up arrow" symbol in the lower left corner of the display. Press the gold shift key again and the symbol goes away. The ■ key is a toggle key that switches back and forth between the "regular" and the "gold" functions. ■ is like the typewriter shift key. After you press ■, look only at gold writing. In this tutorial, whenever you see ■, the label on the next key is the gold label above the key, not the label on the key itself.

Note that the calculator has a continuous memory, so turning it off does not affect any data stored in the calculator.

Clearing the Calculator

To clear the calculator's memory, press ■ [CLEAR ALL].

If we did not press ■, we would input the data shown on the screen to memory. Clearing the calculator is very important, since unwanted data in memory can result in improper calculations, and hence wrong answers. It is best to get into the habit of automatically clearing memory before starting a calculation. Occasionally, you may purposely want to save data, but, in general, you will be entering all new data, so starting with a clear memory is the safest approach.

There are three different levels of clearing data:

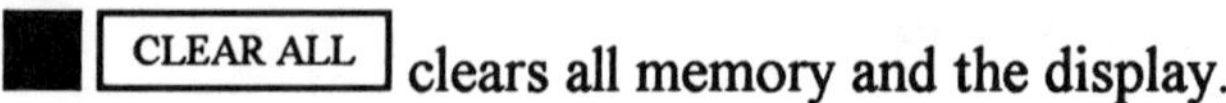

[C] clears the entire display, but not the memory.

[←] clears numbers on the display one at a time if you made a mistake entering data.

Changing the Display

Enter 5555.5555.

To change the number of decimal places from 2 to 4, press ■ [DISP] [4]. 5,555.5555 is displayed.

To change from 4 places to 2, press ■ [DISP] [2]. 5,555.56 is displayed. (Rounding is automatic.)

We usually set the display to 2 places, which is especially convenient when working with dollars and percentages. However, we often use 4 places when dealing with interest rates and rates of return that are entered as decimals.

If periods and commas are reversed, press ■ [./,]. (Many European countries use a ./, convention that is just the opposite of ours.

Note that "PEND" means something is pending. For example, press [4] ÷. The calculator is waiting for the denominator, so "PEND" appears in the display.

Enter [6] and = to get 0.67.

Press ■ [DISP] [4] to see 0.6667.

Press ■ [DISP] [2] to shift back to 2 decimal places.

To control the brightness of the display, hold down [C] and press [+] or [-].

Periods per Year Setting

One important setting that can cause problems is the periods per year setting. To check the current setting, press ■ and then press and hold down [CLEAR ALL]. The display shows the setting for periods/year. The calculator comes pre-set at 12 periods per year, that is, it assumes calculations will be done on a monthly basis. However, finance textbook problems generally use 1 period/year. To change to 1/year:

Press 1 ■ [P/YR].

Now the calculator is set to assume 1 period/year. To confirm this setting, press and hold ■ [CLEAR ALL]. Unless needed for other work, we generally leave the calculator setting at 1 period per year.

Time Value of Money (TVM)

The TVM keys are located on the top row of the keyboard.

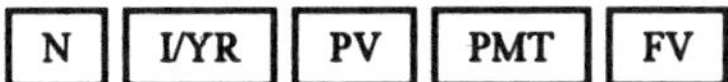

In general, TVM problems involve four variables—three are known and the fourth is unknown.

Lump Sums

To begin, we consider TVM calculations with single (lump) sums. In this situation, we do not use the PMT key, so be sure to either clear all, which sets the payment (PMT) equal to 0, or enter 0 as the PMT when entering the input data. If you know any three variables, you can find the value of the fourth.

Example 1:

What is the FV of $100 after 3 years if the interest rate is 26 percent? First, clear with ■ [CLEAR ALL].

Next, enter the data.

3 [N]

26 [I/YR]

100 [PV]

0 [PMT] (Optional if registers are cleared.)

To determine the FV simply press [FV] and the FV of -$200.04 is displayed.

The HP is programmed so that if the PV is + then the FV is displayed as - and vice versa, because the HP assumes that one is an inflow and the other is an outflow. When entering both PV and FV, one must be entered as negative and the other as positive.

Example 2:

What is the PV of $500 due in 5 years if the interest rate is 10 percent? Clear first and then enter the following data.

5 [N]

10 [I/YR]

0 [PMT] (Optional if registers are cleared.)

500 [FV]

Pressing the [PV] key reveals that $310.46 will grow to $500 in 5 years at a 10 percent rate.

Example 3:

Assume a bond can be purchased today for $200. It will return $1,000 after 14 years. The bond pays no interest during its life. What rate of return would you earn if you bought the bond?

14 [N]

200 [+/-] [PV] (The [+/-] key changes the sign.)

0 [PMT]

1000 [FV]

Simply press the [I/YR] key and the HP calculates the rate of return to be 12.18 percent.

Remember that the HP is programmed so that if the PV is + then the FV is displayed as - and vice versa because the HP assumes that one is an inflow and other is an outflow. When entering both PV and FV values, one must be negative and one positive.

Now suppose you learn that the bond will actually cost $300. What rate of return will you earn?

Override the -200 by entering 300 [+/-] [PV], then press [I/YR] to get 8.98 percent. If you pay more for the bond, you earn less on it. The important thing, though, is that you can do "what if" analyses with the calculator.

Now do nothing except ■ [OFF] to turn off the calculator. Then turn on the calculator [C]. The display shows 0.00. Is the memory erased? Not completely. What was on the screen is gone, but press [RCL] [N] to get N = 14. The other memory registers also retain information unless you press ■ [CLEAR ALL].

Ordinary Annuities

Example 1:

What is the FV of an annuity of $100 paid at the end of each year for 5 years if the interest rate equals 6 percent?

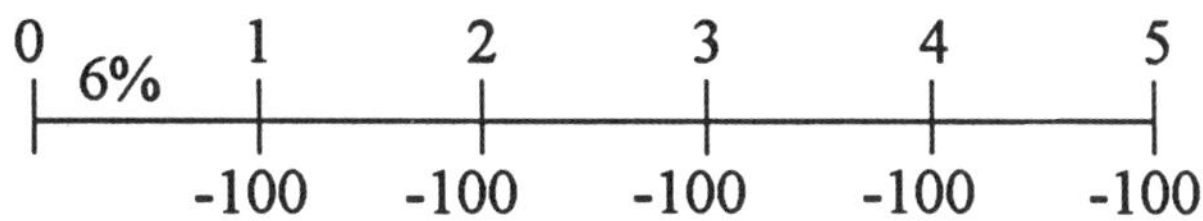

5 [N]

6 [I/YR]

0 [PV]

100 [+/-] [PMT]

Now press the [FV] key, and an FV of $563.71 is displayed.

Example 2:

What is the PV of the same annuity?

Leave data in calculator, but enter 0 as the FV to override, then press [PV] to get \$421.24.

Annuities Due

Each payment of an annuity due occurs at the beginning of the period instead of at the end as with a regular annuity. In essence, each payment is shifted back one period. To analyze annuities due press ■ [BEG/END]. The word "begin" appears on the screen. Now the HP analyzes the cash flows based on beginning of period payments. Change back to end mode by pressing ■ [BEG/END].

Interest Conversion

The following equation is used to convert a nominal rate to an effective rate.

$$\text{EAR} = \left[1 + \frac{k_{\text{Nom}}}{m}\right]^{m} - 1.$$

Given: $k_{\text{Nom}} = 10\%$ and m = 12 payments/year,

$$\text{EAR} = \left[1 + \frac{0.10}{12}\right]^{m} - 1 = (1.0083)^{12} - 1 = 1.1047 - 1 = 0.1047 = 10.47\%.$$

However, it's much easier to convert the nominal rate using the calculator:

10 ■ [NOM %]

12 ■ [P/YR]

■ [EFF %] = 10.47% shows on the screen.

Now switch back to 1 payment/year: 1 ■ [P/YR].

Cash Flow Operations

Example 1: Uneven Cash Flows

Assume the following cash flows:

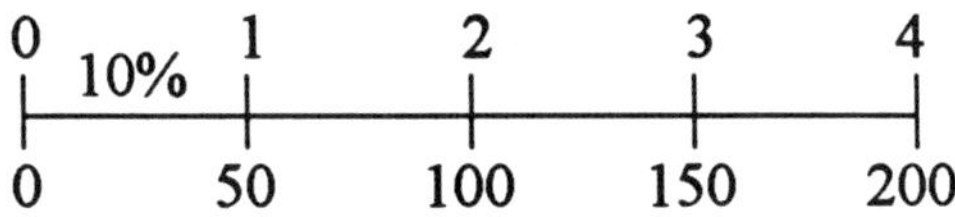

What is the PV of these CFs?

First clear the HP and make sure that periods/year is set equal to 1.

0 [CF_j] Sets CF_0 equal to 0.

50 [CF_j] Sets CF_1 equal to 50. On next entry, hold down CF_j key to see what it says. By holding down CF_j key, you see that you just entered CF_2.

100 [CF_j]

150 [CF_j]

200 [CF_j]

The CFs from the time line are entered. Now enter the interest rate.

10 [I/YR]

At this point the HP knows the cash flows, the number of periods, and the interest rate. To find the PV, press ■ [NPV] to get PV = NPV = $377.40.

Example 2: Embedded Annuities

We have these cash flows, which contain embedded annuities:

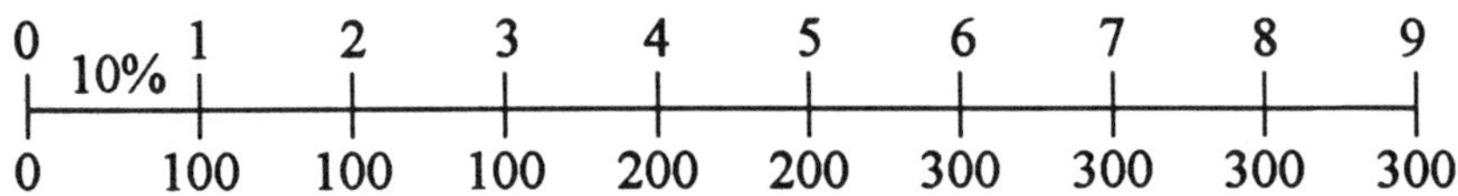

What's the PV?

Clear, set P/YR = 1 if changed.

0 [CF_j]

100 [CF_j]

3 [■] [N_j]

200 [CF_j]

2 [■] [N_j]

300 [CF_j]

4 [■] [N_j]

Now the HP knows the cash flows. Thus, enter the interest rate:

10 [I/YR]

Now press [■] [NPV] to get PV = NPV = $1,099.94.

To check your entries:

[RCL] 0 to see CF_0.

[RCL] [CF_j] to see first CF entry.

[RCL] [■] [N_j] to see how many times CF_1 is repeated, etc.

Example 3: The Rate of Return Offered by an Investment (IRR)[1]

Assume that we invest $1,000 now (t = 0) and then expect to receive an uneven set of cash flows. Here is the CF time line:

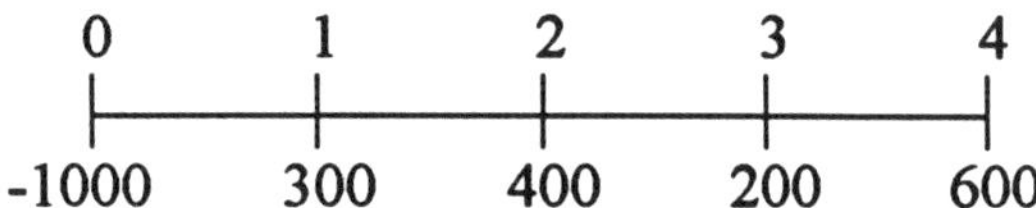

What rate of return will we earn? Enter the following:

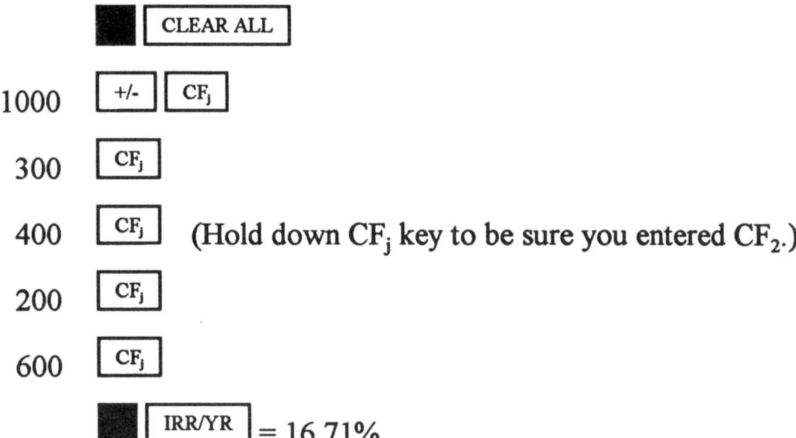

You can also determine the NPV of the investment. Leave data entered and then enter the opportunity cost interest rate, say 8 percent. To find NPV press

8 [I/YR]

■ [NPV]

The NPV of $220.50 is displayed. Thus, the PV of the cash inflows exceeds the cost of the investment by $220.50.

---

[1]If a negative CF occurs at the end of a project's life, then the HP may give an error message, indicating that there are two IRRs. Enter data, then enter 10 ■ [STO] ■ [IRR/YR] to get the first IRR. Then enter a large percentage, such as 100 ■ [STO] ■ [IRR/YR] to find other IRR. You might have to experiment with "guesses" to locate the two IRRs.

Statistical Calculations

The HP can also be used for several types of statistical calculations.

Mean and Standard Deviation (σ)

Year	Sales
1994	$150
1995	95
1996	260

What's the mean (average) and standard deviation (σ) of sales over the 3 years?

Use the Σ+ key to enter data:

150 [Σ+] A number 1 is displayed.

95 [Σ+] A number 2 is displayed.

260 [Σ+] A number 3 is displayed.

Determine the mean and standard deviation by simply pressing

■ [$\bar{x}, \bar{y}$] The mean equals $168.33.

■ [S_x, S_y] The standard deviation is $84.01. S_x and S_y are sample standard deviations. σ_x and σ_y refer to population statistics.

Linear Regression

Beta coefficients can be calculated by using the HP's linear regression capabilities. The X (independent variable) and Y (dependent variable) values must be entered in the proper sequence, where the X data is on the horizontal axis (**market**) and Y data is on the vertical axis (**stock**).

Year	Market (k_M)	Stock (k_j)
1	23.8%	38.6%
2	-7.2	-24.7
3	6.6	12.3
4	20.5	8.2
5	30.6	40.1

Enter the data as follows:

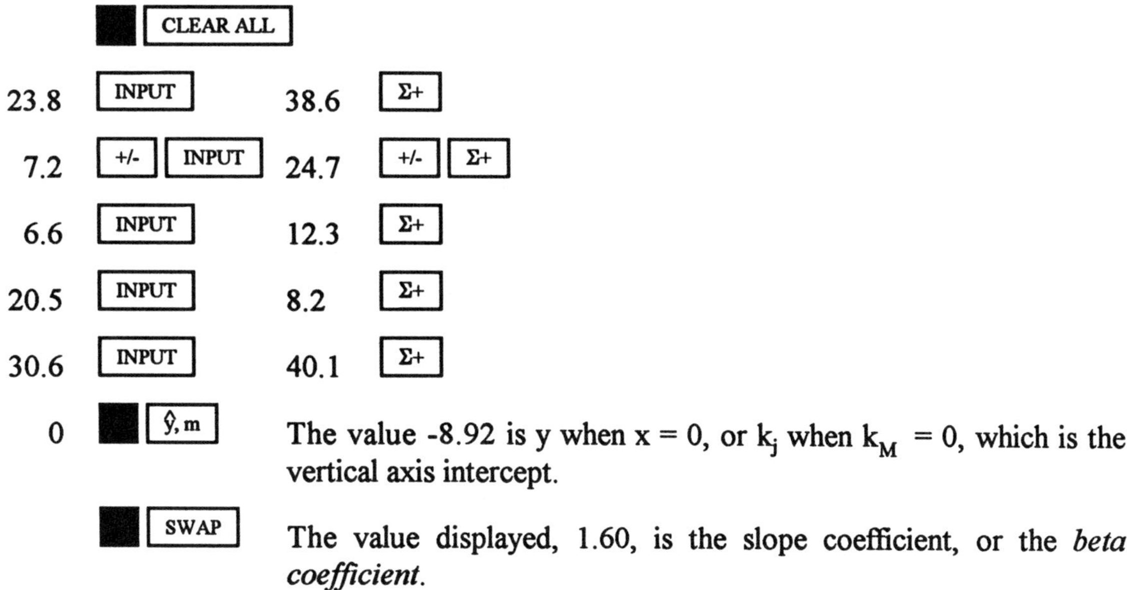

The value -8.92 is y when x = 0, or k_j when k_M = 0, which is the vertical axis intercept.

The value displayed, 1.60, is the slope coefficient, or the *beta coefficient*.

Amortization

The HP can also be used to calculate amortization schedules.

Example:

Determine the interest and principal paid each year and the balance at the end of each year on a three-year $1,000 amortizing loan which carries an interest rate of 10 percent. The payments are due annually.

First, check payments/year and be sure it's 1. Now perform the following steps:

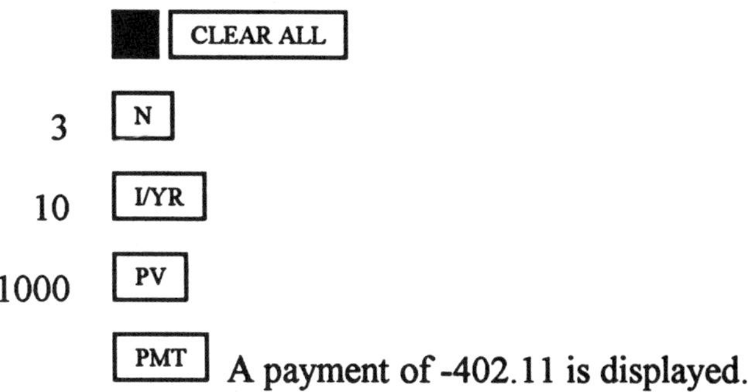

A payment of -402.11 is displayed.

This is the amortization schedule corresponding to the loan.

	Beg. Bal.	Payment	Interest	Princ. Repmt.	Ending Bal.
1	1,000.00	402.11	100.00	302.11	697.89
2	697.89	402.11	69.79	332.32	365.57
3	365.57	402.11	36.56	365.55	.02

With the data still entered in the TVM menu, do the following:

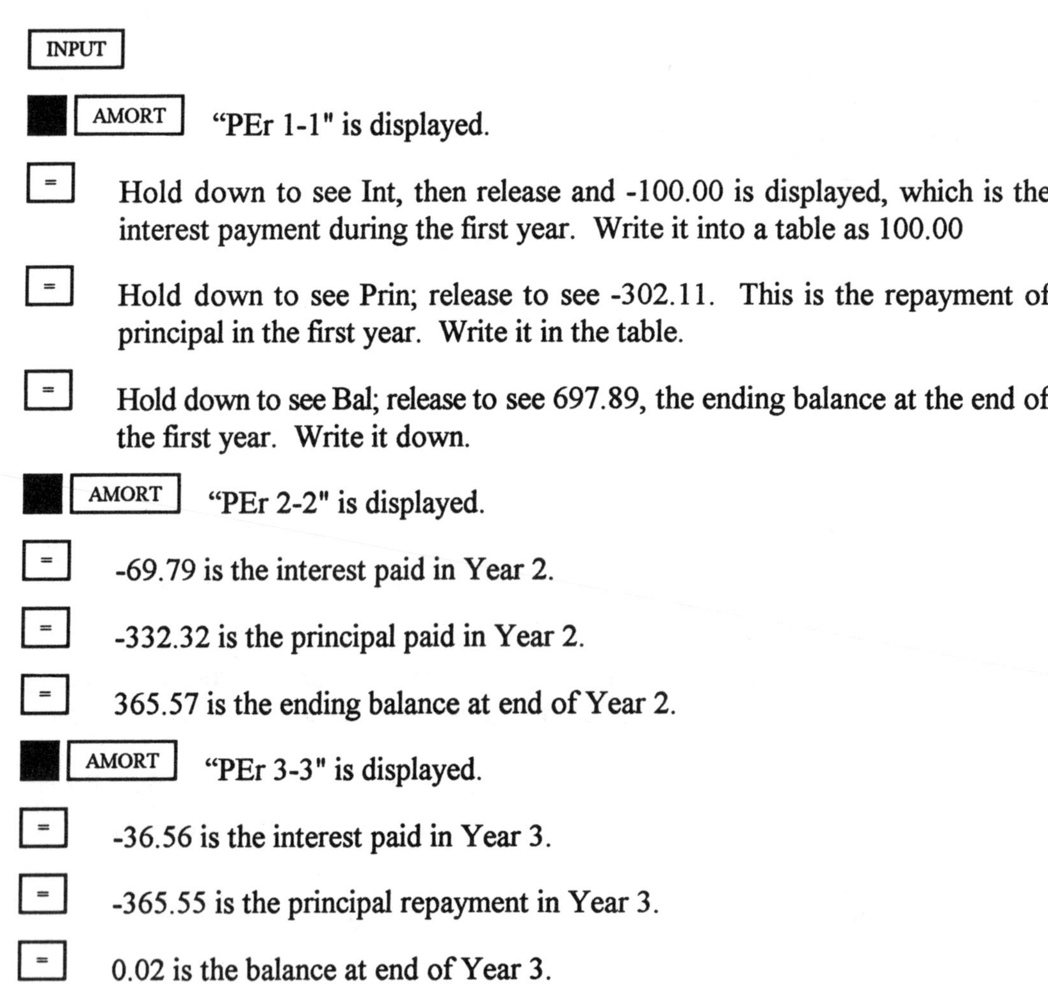

1 INPUT

■ AMORT "PEr 1-1" is displayed.

= Hold down to see Int, then release and -100.00 is displayed, which is the interest payment during the first year. Write it into a table as 100.00

= Hold down to see Prin; release to see -302.11. This is the repayment of principal in the first year. Write it in the table.

= Hold down to see Bal; release to see 697.89, the ending balance at the end of the first year. Write it down.

■ AMORT "PEr 2-2" is displayed.

= -69.79 is the interest paid in Year 2.

= -332.32 is the principal paid in Year 2.

= 365.57 is the ending balance at end of Year 2.

■ AMORT "PEr 3-3" is displayed.

= -36.56 is the interest paid in Year 3.

= -365.55 is the principal repayment in Year 3.

= 0.02 is the balance at end of Year 3.

See the manual for an explanation of how to do monthly amortization.

Next, with the data still in the calculator, do the following:

1 [INPUT] 3 ■ [AMORT] "PEr 1-3" is displayed.

[=] Hold down to see Int, then release and -206.35 displayed. This is the total interest paid over Years 1 to 3.

[=] Hold down to see Prin, then release and -999.98 is displayed. This is the total repayment of principal over Years 1 to 3.

[=] Hold down to see Bal, then release and 0.02 is displayed. This is the remaining balance.

Hewlett-Packard 12C Tutorial

To begin, look at the face of the calculator. Every key (except the arithmetic function keys in the far right column and the five keys on the bottom left row) has two or three functions: each key's primary function is noted in white on the key itself, while each key's secondary function is noted in gold above the key or in blue on the lower face of the key. To use the function on the key, simply press the key. To access the gold function above each key, first press the gold [f] key, which we will call the "gold shift" key, and then press the desired function key. (Note that the gold shift key is near the lower left corner of the calculator keyboard.) To access the blue function on the bottom of each key, first press the blue [g] key, which we will call the "blue shift" key, and then press the desired function. (The blue shift key is located just to the right of the gold shift key.)

Turning the Calculator On and Off

To turn on the calculator, press [ON].

Note that the ON key is on the lower left corner of the keyboard—the face of the key has a white "ON". Also, we will designate keys throughout this tutorial by the use of small boxes, as above. To conserve the battery, the calculator turns itself off about 10 minutes after your last keystroke.

To turn the calculator off, press [ON] again.

Also, note that pressing the gold shift key places a little "f" in the lower left corner of the display. Pressing the blue shift key places a little "g" at the bottom of the display. Press the [CLX] key and the symbol goes away. The shift keys are toggle keys that switch back and forth between the "regular" and the "gold" or "blue" functions. They are like the typewriter shift key. After you press the "gold" (or "blue") key, look only at gold (or blue) writing.

Note that the calculator has a continuous memory, so turning it off does not affect any data stored in the calculator.

Clearing the Calculator

Clearing the calculator is very important, since unwanted data in memory can result in improper calculations, and hence wrong answers. It is best to get into the habit of automatically clearing memory before starting a calculation. Occasionally, you may purposely want to save data, but, in general, you will be entering all new data, so starting with a clear memory is the safest approach.

There are four different levels of clearing data:

[f] [REG] clears all memory and the display.

[CLX] clears the entire display, but not the memory.

[f] [FIN] clears the financial register but not the display.

[f] [Σ] clears the statistics register and the display.

Note that the keys above are designated as CLEAR keys on the face of the calculator.

Changing the Display

Enter 5555.5555.

To change decimals from 2 to 4, press [f] [4]. 5,555.5555 is displayed.

To change from 4 places to 2, press [f] [2]. 5,555.56 is displayed. (Rounding is automatic.)

We usually set the display to 2 places, which is especially convenient when working with dollars and percentages. However, we often use 4 places when dealing with interest rates and rates of return that are entered as decimals.

Time Value of Money (TVM)

The TVM keys are located on the top row of the keyboard.

[n] [i] [PV] [PMT] [FV]

In general, TVM problems involve four variables—three are known and the fourth is unknown.

Lump Sums

To begin, we consider TVM calculations with single (lump) sums. In this situation, we do not use the PMT key, so be sure to either clear all, which sets the payment (PMT) equal to 0, or enter 0 as the PMT when entering the input data. If you know any three variables, you can find the value of the fourth.

Example 1:

What is the FV of $100 after 3 years if the interest rate is 26 percent? First, clear with [f] [FIN].

Next, enter the data.

3 [n]

26 [i]

100 [PV]

0 [PMT] (Optional if registers are cleared.)

To determine the FV simply press [FV] and the FV of -$200.04 is displayed.

The HP is programmed so that if the PV is + then the FV is displayed as - and vice versa, because the HP assumes that one is an inflow and the other is an outflow. When entering both PV and FV, one must be entered as negative and the other positive.

Example 2:

What is the PV of $500 due in 5 years if the interest rate is 10 percent? Clear first and then enter the following data:

5 [n]

10 [i]

0 [PMT] (Optional if registers are cleared.)

500 [FV]

Pressing the [PV] key reveals that $310.46 will grow to $500 in 5 years at a 10 percent rate.

Example 3:

Assume a bond can be purchased today for $200. It will return $1,000 after 14 years. The bond pays no interest during its life. What rate of return would you earn if you bought the bond?

14 [n]

200 [CHS] [PV] (The [CHS] key changes the sign.)

0 [PMT]

1000 [FV]

Simply press the [i] key and the HP calculates the rate of return to be 12.18 percent.

Remember that the HP is programmed so that if the PV is + then the FV is displayed as - and vice versa, because the HP assumes that one value is an inflow and other is an outflow. Also note that the negative sign is placed on the 200 PV entry by pressing the key marked "CHS" for change sign.

Now suppose you learn that the bond will actually cost $300. What rate of return will you earn?

Override the -200 by entering 300 [CHS] [PV], then press [i] to get 8.98 percent. If you pay more for the bond, you earn less on it. The important thing, though, is that you can do "what if" analyses with the calculator.

Now press [ON] to turn off the calculator. Then turn on the calculator [ON]. The display still shows 8.98. The memory is not erased. What was on the screen when you turned the calculator off returns when you turn it back on. Now press [CLX]. What was on the screen is gone, but press [RCL] [n] to get N = 14. The other memory registers also retain information unless you press [f] [FIN].

Ordinary Annuities

Example 1:

What is the FV of an annuity of $100 paid at the end of each year for 5 years if the interest rate equals 6 percent?

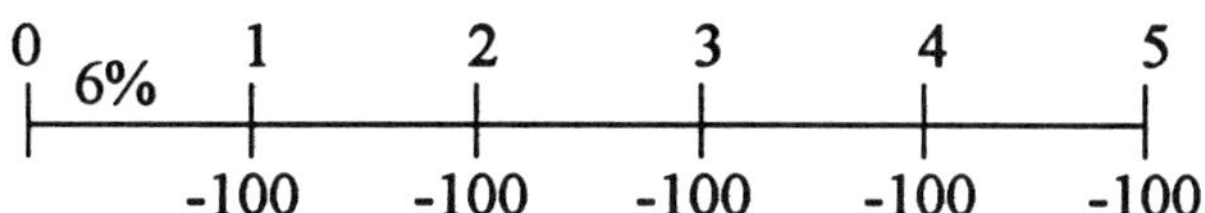

5 [n]

6 [i]

0 [PV]

100 [CHS] [PMT]

Now press the [FV] key, and an FV of $563.71 is displayed.

Example 2:

What is the PV of the same annuity?

Leave data in calculator, but enter 0 as the FV to override, then press [PV] to get $421.24.

Annuities Due

Each payment of an annuity due occurs at the beginning of the period instead of at the end as with a regular annuity. In essence, each payment is shifted back one period. To analyze annuities due press [g] [BEG]. The word "BEGIN" appears on the screen. Now the HP analyzes the cash flows based on beginning of period payments. Change back to end mode by pressing [g] [END].

Interest Conversion

The following equation is used to convert a nominal rate to an effective rate.

$$EAR = \left[1 + \frac{k_{Nom}}{m}\right]^m - 1.$$

Given: $k_{Nom} = 10\%$ and $m = 12$ payments/year,

$$EAR = \left[1 + \frac{0.10}{12}\right]^m - 1 = (1.0083)^{12} - 1 = 1.1047 - 1 = 0.1047 = 10.47\%.$$

However, it's much easier to convert the nominal rate using the calculator:

First, clear the financial register, [f] [FIN].

10 [ENTER]

12 [n] [÷] [i]

[CHS] [PMT] [FV] 10.47% shows on the screen.

Cash Flow Operations

We can also find the PV, FV, and IRR (rate of return) of a series of unequal cash flows.

Example 1: Uneven Cash Flows

Assume the following cash flows:

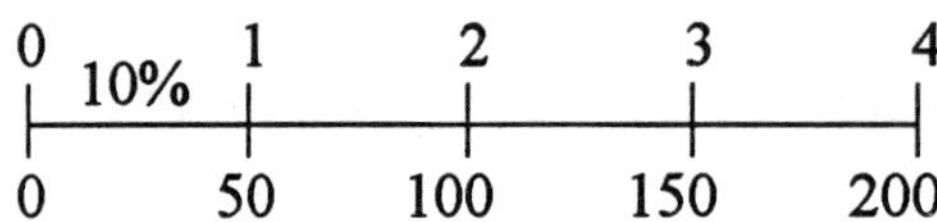

What is the PV of these CFs?

First clear the HP's financial register, [f] [FIN].

0 [g] [CF_0] Sets CF_0 equal to 0.

50 [g] [CF_j] Sets CF_1 equal to 50.

100 [g] [CF_j]

150 [g] [CF_j]

200 [g] [CF_j]

The CFs from the time line are entered. Now enter the interest rate:

10 [i]

At this point the HP knows the cash flows, the number of periods, and the interest rate. To find the PV, press [f] [NPV] to get PV = NPV = $377.40.

Example 2: Embedded Annuities

We have these cash flows, which contain embedded annuities:

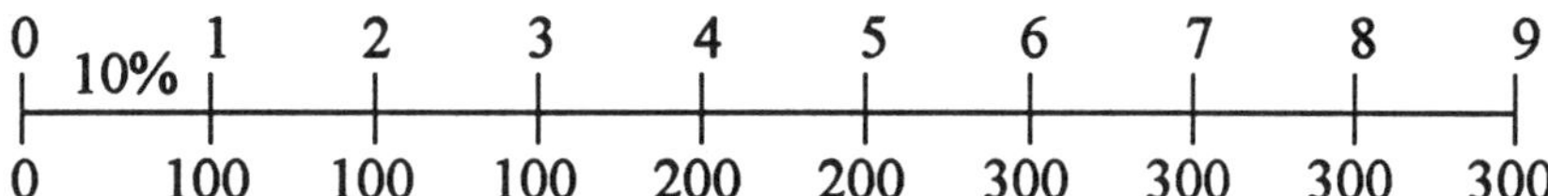

What's the PV?

Clear the HP, [f] [FIN].

0 [g] [CF_0]

100 [g] [CF_j]

3 [g] [N_j]

200 [g] [CF_j]

2 [g] [N_j]

300 [g] [CF_j]

4 [g] [N_j]

Now the HP knows the cash flows. Thus, enter the interest rate:

10 [i]

Now press [f] [NPV] to get PV = NPV = $1,099.94.

To check your entries:

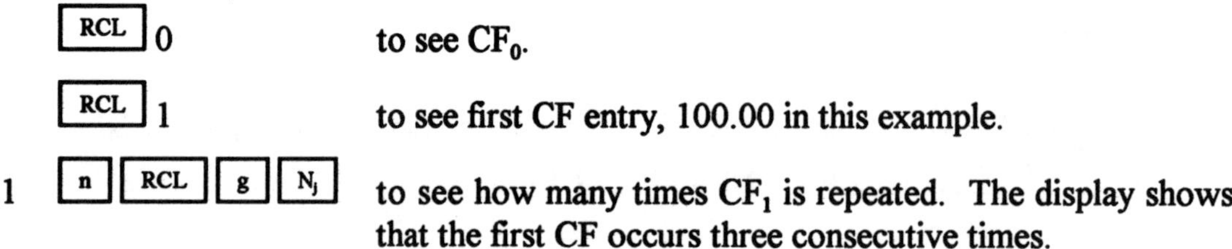

to see CF_0.

to see first CF entry, 100.00 in this example.

to see how many times CF_1 is repeated. The display shows that the first CF occurs three consecutive times.

Example 3: The Rate of Return Offered by an Investment (IRR)[1]

Assume that we invest $1,000 now (t = 0) and then expect to receive an uneven set of cash flows. Here is the CF time line:

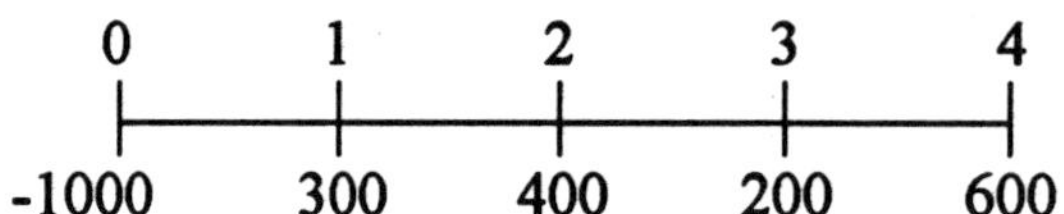

What rate of return will we earn? Enter the following:

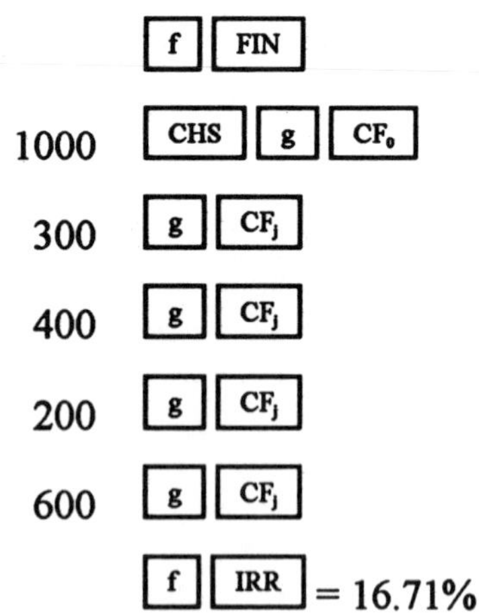

= 16.71%

---

[1]If a negative CF occurs at the end of a project's life, then the HP may give an error message, indicating that there are two IRRs. Enter data, then enter 10 ENTER and then RCL g R/S to get the first IRR. Then enter a large percentage, such as 100 ENTER and then RCL g R/S to find the other IRR. You might have to experiment with "guesses" to locate the two IRRs.

You can also determine the NPV of the investment. Leave data entered and then enter the opportunity cost interest rate, say 8 percent. To find NPV press:

8 [i] [f] [NPV]

The NPV of $220.50 is displayed. Thus, the PV of the cash inflows exceeds the cost of the investment by $220.50.

Statistical Calculations

The HP can also be used for several types of statistical calculations.

Mean and Standard Deviation (σ)

Year	Sales
1994	$150
1995	95
1996	260

What's the mean (average) and standard deviation (σ) of sales over the 3 years?

Use the Σ+ key to enter data:

[f] [Σ]	Clears the statistical register.
150 [Σ+]	A number 1 is displayed.
95 [Σ+]	A number 2 is displayed.
260 [Σ+]	A number 3 is displayed.

Determine the mean and standard deviation by simply pressing

[g] [$\bar{X}$]	The mean equals $168.33.
[g] [S]	The standard deviation is $84.01. S is the sample standard deviation.

Linear Regression

Beta coefficients can be calculated by using the HP's linear regression capabilities. The X (independent variable) and Y (dependent variable) values must be entered in the proper sequence, where X data is on the horizontal axis (**market**) and Y data is on the vertical axis (**stock**).

Year	Market (k_M)	Stock (k_j)
1	23.8%	38.6%
2	-7.2	-24.7
3	6.6	12.3
4	20.5	8.2
5	30.6	40.1

Enter the data as follows:

[f] [Σ]

Note: The order in which the data is entered is very important. The Y value (k_j) must be entered before the X value (k_M).

38.6 [ENTER] 23.8 [Σ+]

24.7 [CHS] [ENTER] 7.2 [CHS] [Σ+]

12.3 [ENTER] 6.6 [Σ+]

8.2 [ENTER] 20.5 [Σ+]

40.1 [ENTER] 30.6 [Σ+]

0 [g] [ŷ,r] The value -8.92 is y when x = 0, or k_j when k_M = 0, which is the *vertical axis intercept*.

[STO] [0] Stores the value of the Y intercept for use in calculating the slope (beta).

0 [g] [x̂,r] 5.57 is the value of x when y = 0.

[RCL] 0 [CHS] [X≷Y] [÷] The value displayed, 1.60, is the slope coefficient, or the *beta coefficient*.

Amortization

The HP can also be used to calculate amortization schedules.

Example:

Determine the interest and principal paid each year and the balance at the end of each year on a three-year $1,000 amortizing loan which carries an interest rate of 10 percent. The payments are due annually.

Perform the following steps:

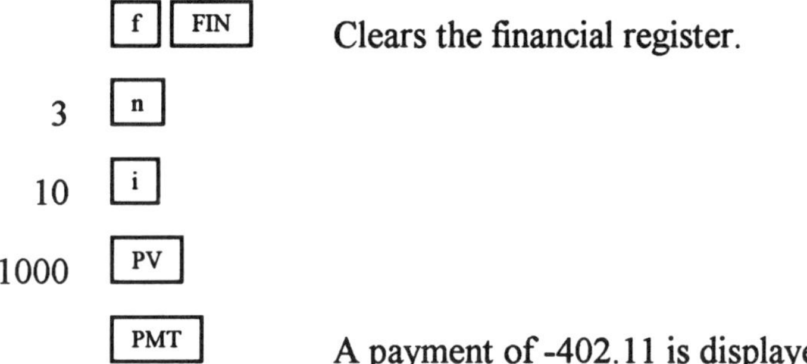

Clears the financial register.

A payment of -402.11 is displayed.

This is the amortization schedule corresponding to the loan.

	Beg. Bal.	Payment	Interest	Princ. Repmt.	Ending Bal.
1	1,000.00	402.11	100.00	302.11	697.89
2	697.89	402.11	69.79	332.32	365.57
3	365.57	402.11	36.56	365.55	.02

With the data still entered in the TVM menu, do the following:

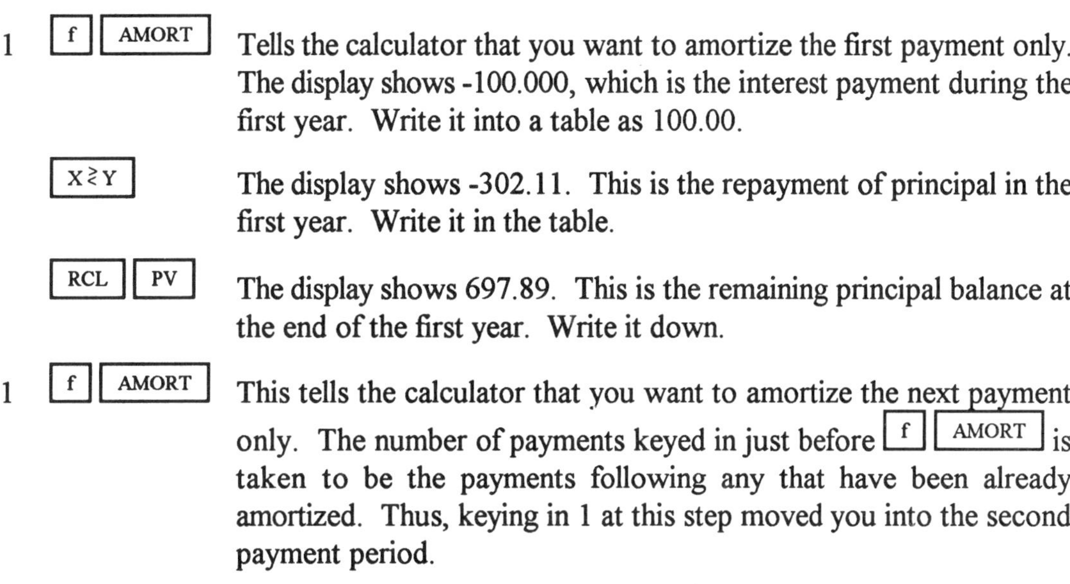

Tells the calculator that you want to amortize the first payment only. The display shows -100.000, which is the interest payment during the first year. Write it into a table as 100.00.

The display shows -302.11. This is the repayment of principal in the first year. Write it in the table.

The display shows 697.89. This is the remaining principal balance at the end of the first year. Write it down.

This tells the calculator that you want to amortize the next payment only. The number of payments keyed in just before f AMORT is taken to be the payments following any that have been already amortized. Thus, keying in 1 at this step moved you into the second payment period.

-69.79 is the interest paid in Year 2.

	[X≷Y]	-332.32 is the principal paid in Year 2.
	[RCL] [PV]	365.57 is the ending balance at end of Year 2.
1	[f] [AMORT]	-35.56 is the interest paid in Year 3.
	[X≷Y]	-365.55 is the principal repayment in Year 3.
	[RCL] [PV]	0.02 is the balance at end of Year 3.

See the manual for an explanation of how to do monthly amortization.

Next, with the data still in the calculator, do the following:

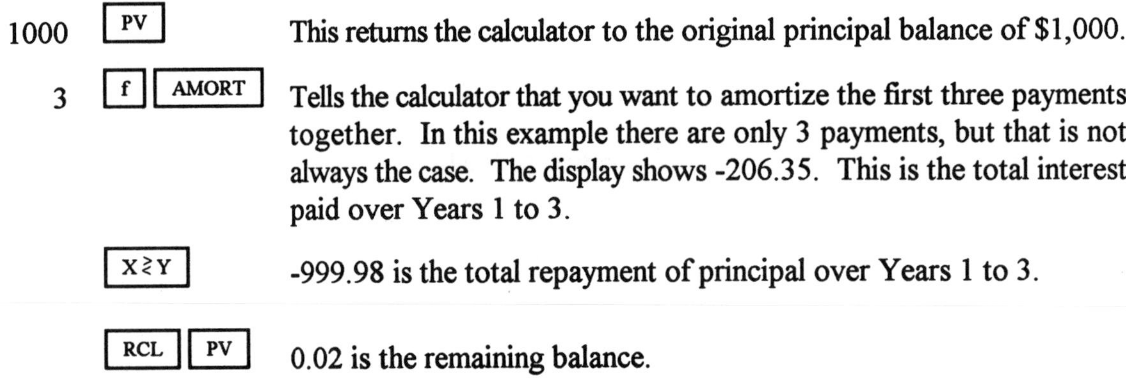

1000	[PV]	This returns the calculator to the original principal balance of $1,000.
3	[f] [AMORT]	Tells the calculator that you want to amortize the first three payments together. In this example there are only 3 payments, but that is not always the case. The display shows -206.35. This is the total interest paid over Years 1 to 3.
	[X≷Y]	-999.98 is the total repayment of principal over Years 1 to 3.
	[RCL] [PV]	0.02 is the remaining balance.

Hewlett-Packard 17BII Tutorial

To begin, look at the face of the calculator. Most keys on the 17BII have two functions: a key's primary function is noted in white on the key itself, while the key's secondary function is noted in gold above the key. To use the function on the key, simply press the key. To access the gold function above each key, first press the key with the solid gold face, which we will call the "gold shift" key, and then press the desired function key. (Note that the gold shift key is near the lower left corner of the calculator keyboard.)

Turning the Calculator On and Off

To turn on the calculator, press [CLR].

Note that the ON key is on the lower left corner of the keyboard—the face of the key has a white "CLR," while the word "ON" appears below the key. Also, we will designate keys throughout this tutorial by the use of small boxes, as above. To conserve the battery, the calculator turns itself off about 10 minutes after your last keystroke.

To turn the calculator off, press ■ [OFF].

Here we are using the solid black square to represent the gold shift key. Thus, the keystrokes to turn the calculator off are (1) press the gold shift key, and (2) then press the CLR key. Note that the word "OFF" appears above the CLR key in gold. Thus, by pressing the gold shift key first, we are activating the gold function above the CLR key, which is the off function. Also, note that pressing the gold shift key places a little "up arrow" symbol in the upper left corner of the display. Press the gold shift key again and the symbol goes away. The ■ key is a toggle key that switches back and forth between the "regular" and the "gold" functions. ■ is like the typewriter shift key. After you press ■, look only at the gold writing.

Note that the calculator has a continuous memory, so turning it off does not affect any data stored in the calculator.

The Menu System

The HP17BII differs from many calculators in that it uses a menu system. To access the main menu, press ■ [MAIN]. The display shows five menu choices: FIN, BUS, SUM, TIME, and SOLVE. To access one of the menu choices, press the arrowhead key directly below the appropriate choice. To illustrate, press the arrowhead key directly below FIN. (We will designate this operation by [FIN]. Thus, a shaded box means press one of the arrowhead keys rather than one of the regular keys.) Now

a new set of menu choices appears. Press [TVM] to get into the time value of money menu. To get back to the main menu, either press ■ [MAIN] or press [EXIT] a number of times until the menu items stop changing.

Clearing the Calculator

To clear the calculator's memory, press ■ [CLEAR DATA].

Clearing the calculator is very important, since unwanted data in memory can result in improper calculations, and hence wrong answers. It is best to get into the habit of automatically clearing memory before starting a calculation. Occasionally, you may purposely want to save data, but, in general, you will be entering all new data, so starting with a clear memory is the safest approach.

There are three different levels of clearing data:

> ■ [CLEAR DATA] clears all memory and the display.
>
> [CLR] clears the entire display, but not the memory.
>
> [←] clears numbers on the display one at a time if you made a mistake entering data.

Changing the Display

To change the number of decimal places from 2 to 4, press [DSP] [FIX] [4] [INPUT]. Now press 5555.5555 [INPUT]. 5,555.5555 is displayed.

Note that the calculator display itself is often used to designate calculator functions. When this occurs, we shade the box as above. To invoke the function displayed, press the arrowhead key directly below the function.

To change from 4 places to 2, press [DSP] [FIX] [2] [INPUT]. Now press 5555.5555 [INPUT]. 5,555.56 is displayed. (Rounding is automatic.)

We usually set the display to 2 places, which is especially convenient when working with dollars and percentages. However, we often use 4 places when dealing with interest rates and rates of return that are entered as decimals.

To control the brightness of the display, hold down [CLR] and press [+] or [-].

Periods per Year Setting

One important setting that can cause problems is the periods per year setting. To check the current setting, first press [■] [MAIN] to get the main menu, and then press [FIN] [TVM]. The display shows the setting for periods/year. The calculator comes pre-set at 12 periods per year, that is, it assumes calculations will be done on a monthly basis. However, the problems in finance textbooks generally use 1 period/year. To change to 1/year:

1) From the main menu, press [FIN] [TVM] [OTHER] [1] [P/YR].
2) Return to the main menu by pressing [EXIT] three times or [■] [MAIN].

Time Value of Money (TVM)

To enter the time value of money menu, do the following:

From the main menu, press [FIN] [TVM].

In general, TVM problems involve four variables—three are known and the fourth is unknown.

Lump Sums

To begin, we consider TVM calculations with single (lump) sums. In this situation, we do not have payments, so be sure to either press [CLEAR DATA], which sets the payment (PMT) equal to 0, or enter 0 for the PMT. If you know any three variables, you can find the value of the fourth.

Example 1:

What is the FV of $100 after 3 years if the interest rate is 26 percent? First, clear with ■ CLEAR DATA and enter the following data:

3 N

26 I%YR

100 PV

0 PMT (Optional if registers are cleared.)

Next, press FV and the future value of -$200.04 is displayed.

The HP is programmed so that if the PV is + then the FV is displayed as - and vice versa, because the HP assumes that one is an inflow and the other is an outflow. If you are entering both PV and FV, one must be entered as negative and the other positive.

Example 2:

What is the PV of $500 due in 5 years if the interest rate is 10 percent? Clear data first and then enter the following:

5 N

10 I%YR

0 PMT (Optional if registers are cleared.)

500 FV

Next, press PV and the present value of -$310.46 is displayed. Thus, $310.46 will grow to $500 in 5 years at a 10 percent rate.

Example3:

Assume a bond can be purchased today for $200. It will return $1,000 after 14 years. The bond pays no interest during its life. What rate of return would you earn if you bought the bond?

14 [N]

200 [+/-] [PV] (The [+/-] key changes the sign.)

0 [PMT]

1000 [FV]

Next, press [I%YR] and a rate of return of 12.18 percent is displayed.

Remember to press [+/-] to convert the 200 to -200 because the purchase of the bond is a cash outflow!

Now suppose you learn that the bond will actually cost $300. What rate of return will you earn?

Override the -200 by simply entering 300 [+/-] [PV] and then press [I%YR] to get 8.98 percent. If you pay more for the bond, you earn less on it. The important thing, though, is that you can do "what if" analyses with the calculator.

Ordinary Annuities

Now we will use the PMT key, and either the PV or the FV key, depending on whether we want to find the PV or the FV of the annuity.

Example 1:

What is the FV of an annuity of $100 paid at the end of each year for 5 years if the interest rate equals 6 percent?

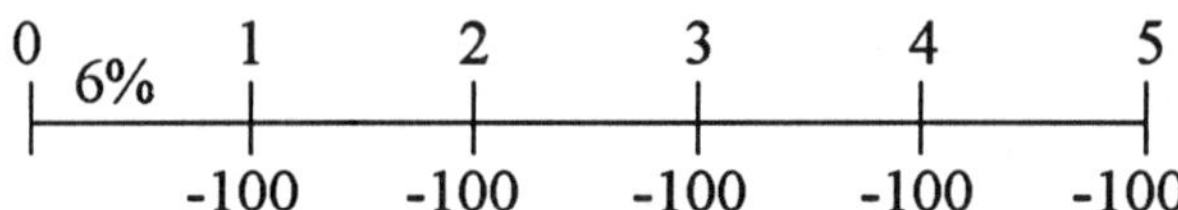

5 [N]

6 [I%YR]

0 [PV]

100 [+/-] [PMT]

Now press the [FV] key, and an FV of $563.71 is displayed.

Example 2:

What is the PV of the same annuity?

Leave data in calculator, but enter 0 as the FV to override, then press [PV] to get $421.24.

Annuities Due

Each payment of an annuity due occurs at the beginning of the period instead of at the end as with a regular annuity. In essence, each payment is shifted back one period. To analyze annuities due press [FIN] [TVM] [OTHER] [BEG]. The words "BEGIN MODE" appear on the screen. Now the HP analyzes the cash flows based on beginning of period payments. Change back to end mode by pressing [END]. To get back to the TVM menu press [EXIT].

Interest Conversion

The following equation is used to convert a nominal rate to an effective rate.

$$\text{EAR} = \left[1 + \frac{k_{\text{Nom}}}{m}\right]^m - 1.$$

Given: $k_{Nom} = 10\%$ and m = 12 payments/year,

$$EAR = \left[1 + \frac{0.10}{12}\right]^{m} - 1 = (1.0083)^{12} - 1 = 1.1047 - 1 = 0.1047 = 10.47\%.$$

This formula is fine, however, the calculator can be used to convert the rates much faster.

From the main menu press [FIN] [ICNV] [PER].

Now, enter 12 and then press [P] to compound 12 times per year.

To enter 10 percent as the nominal rate, press 10 [NOM %].

Now, to determine the effective rate simply press [EFF %] and 10.47 percent is displayed.

Cash Flow Operations

The HP is useful for finding the PV, FV, and IRR (rate of return) of a series of unequal cash flows.

Example 1: Uneven Cash Flows

Assume the following cash flows:

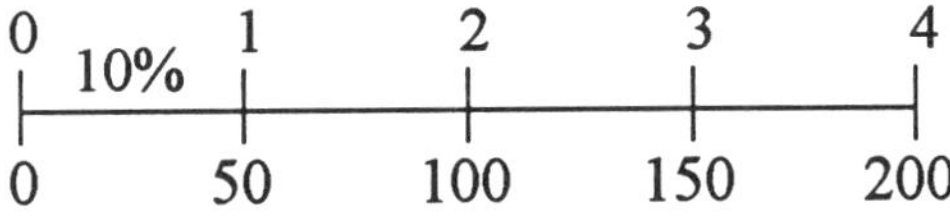

What is the PV of these CFs? Clear the memory by pressing ■ [CLEAR DATA].

You should also clear any previously entered cash flow lists by pressing [FIN] [CFLO] ■ [CLEAR DATA] [YES].

Now, press [#T?] until "#TIMES PROMPTING: OFF" is displayed because each cash flow is different than the one before it and thus occurs only one time. There is no need for the HP to prompt you for the number of times that a particular cash flow occurs since each one is different than the one before it.

The screen should now display "FLOW(0)=?". Next, enter the following:

0	INPUT	This enters 0 as the cash flow at time 0.
50	INPUT	This enters 50 as the CF_1.
100	INPUT	This enters 100 as the CF_2.
150	INPUT	This enters 150 as the CF_3.
200	INPUT	This enters 200 as the CF_4.

After all the cash flows have been entered, press EXIT to return to the menu. Select CALC and "NPV, NUS, NFV NEED I%" is displayed.

Now enter the 10 percent interest rate by pressing 10 I%.

At this point the HP knows the cash flows, the number of periods, and the interest rate. To find the NPV, press NPV to get PV = NPV = $377.40.

Example 2: Embedded Annuities

Assume the following cash flows, which contain embedded annuities or groups of equal, consecutive cash flows:

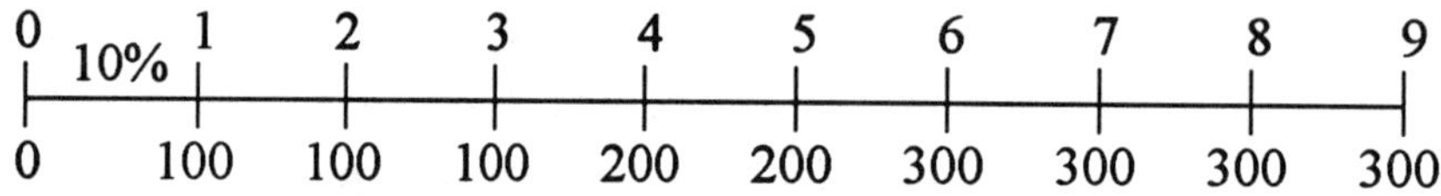

What's the PV?

Clear the previously entered cash flow lists by pressing FIN CFLO ■ CLEAR DATA YES from the main menu.

Now enter #T? until "#TIMES PROMPTING: ON" is displayed. After each cash flow is entered the calculator will prompt you for the number of times that cash flow occurs. This feature saves you from having to enter identical, consecutive cash flows one by one. If each cash flow is different than the one before it (see previous example), then the "#TIMES PROMPTING" can be turned off.

The screen should now display "FLOW(0)=?".

Next enter the cash flows.

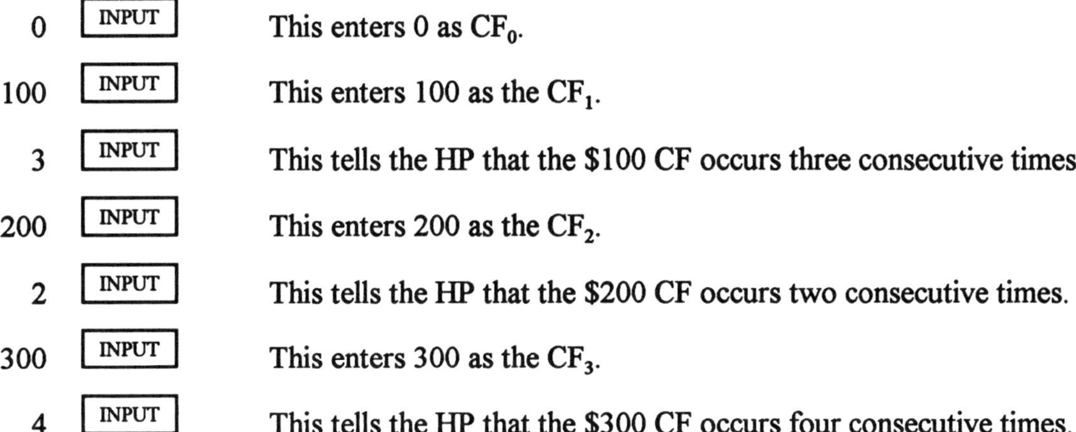

0	INPUT	This enters 0 as CF_0.
100	INPUT	This enters 100 as the CF_1.
3	INPUT	This tells the HP that the $100 CF occurs three consecutive times.
200	INPUT	This enters 200 as the CF_2.
2	INPUT	This tells the HP that the $200 CF occurs two consecutive times.
300	INPUT	This enters 300 as the CF_3.
4	INPUT	This tells the HP that the $300 CF occurs four consecutive times.

After all the cash flows have been entered, press EXIT to return to the menu. Select CALC and "NPV, NUS, NFV NEED I%" is displayed.

Now enter the 10 percent interest rate by pressing 10 I%.

At this point the HP knows the cash flows, the number of periods, and the interest rate. To find the NPV, press NPV to get PV = NPV = $1,099.94.

Lastly, the ▲ and ▼ keys can be used to view your cash flow list entries. First, exit to the menu that looks like this:

CALC | INSR | DELET | NAME | GET | #T?

Then simply use the ▲ and ▼ keys to view the cash flow entries.

Example 3: The Rate of Return Offered by an Investment (IRR)[1]

Assume that we invest $1,000 now (t = 0) and then expect to receive an uneven set of cash flows.

---

[1]If a negative CF occurs at the end of a project's life, then the HP may give an error message, indicating that there are two IRRs. Enter data, then enter 10 STO IRR to get the first IRR. Then enter a large percentage, such as 100 STO IRR to find the other IRR. You might have to experiment with "guesses" to locate the two IRRs.

Here is the CF time line:

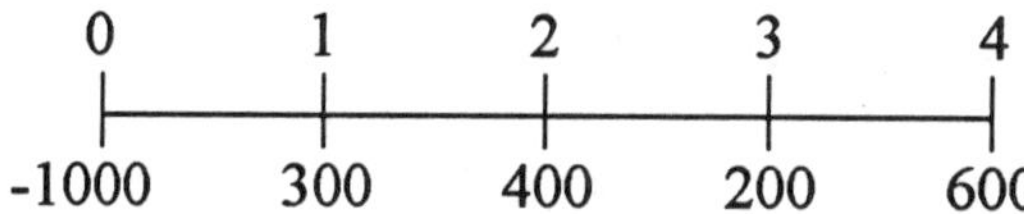

What rate of return will we earn?

Clear the previously entered cash flow lists by pressing [FIN] [CFLO] [■] [CLEAR DATA] [YES]. Now press [#T?] until the "#TIMES PROMPTING" is turned off.

Now enter the cash flows as follows:

1000 [+/-] [INPUT]

300 [INPUT]

400 [INPUT]

200 [INPUT]

600 [INPUT]

After all the cash flows have been entered, press [EXIT] to return to the menu. Select [CALC] and "NPV, NUS, NFV NEED I%" is displayed.

Now enter the 10 percent interest rate by pressing 10 [I%].

At this point the HP knows the cash flows, the number of periods, and the interest rate.

To find the IRR, press [IRR%] to get IRR = 16.71%.

You can also determine the NPV of the investment. Leave data entered and then enter the opportunity cost interest rate, say 8 percent. To find NPV press:

8 [I%] [NPV]

The NPV of $220.50 is displayed. Thus, the PV of the cash inflows exceeds the cost of the investment by $220.50.

Statistical Calculations

The HP can also be used for several types of statistical calculations.

Mean and Standard Deviation (σ)

Year	Sales
1994	$150
1995	95
1996	260

What's the mean (average) and standard deviation (σ) of sales over the 3 years?

The first step is to enter the data into a sum list. From the main menu press [SUM].

Clear any previously entered sum lists by next pressing:

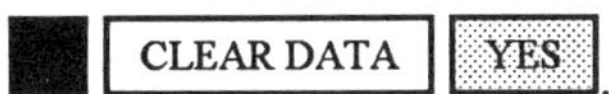

"ITEM(1)=?" is displayed.

Enter the sales data into the sum list as follows:

150 [INPUT]

95 [INPUT]

260 [INPUT]

Now press [EXIT] to return to the menu and then press [CALC] to display the following menu:

Press [MEAN] and the mean of $168.33 is displayed.

Press [STDEV] and the standard deviation of $84.01 is displayed.

Linear Regression

Beta coefficients can be calculated by using the HP's linear regression capabilities. The X (independent variable) and Y (dependent variable) values must be entered in the proper sequence, where the X data is on the horizontal axis **(market)** and Y data is on the vertical axis **(stock)**.

Year	Market (k_M)	Stock (k_j)
1	23.8%	38.6%
2	-7.2	-24.7
3	6.6	12.3
4	20.5	8.2
5	30.6	40.1

Enter the data as follows.

To clear any previously entered list, from the main menu, press:

First we must create two sum lists: one for the x-values and one for the y-values. Each list must have the same number of items.

To create a sum list for the x-values do the following:

Enter the five X variables:

23.8 INPUT

7.2 +/- INPUT

6.6 INPUT

20.5 INPUT

30.6 INPUT

Now we must store this list under a name before we create another sum list for the Y variables. Store the X variable sum list as follows:

The HP now asks you to input a name for the sum list. We will name the list "X" by pressing:

[WXYZ] [X] [INPUT] Of course you could have named the list any name that sufficiently describes the contents of the list (market return) such as KM or MKRT.

We have just created a sum list names "X", which contains the five X variables.

The display now shows "ITEM(6)=?" but we need to create a sum list for the Y variables starting with Item(1). To create a new sum list for Y, start a new list as follows:

[GET] [*NEW] This tells the HP to start a new sum list.

Now simply enter the Y variables and name the list "Y" just as you did for the X variables above.

Next, press [CALC] [MORE] [FRCST].

At this time, the HP asks you to select the X variable from the lists we created:

Press [X] to select the list named "X" and press [Y] to select the list named "Y" as the Y variable.

Next, we must select the curve-fitting model we want to use by pressing:

[MORE] [MODL] [LIN].

To calculate the curve-fitting results, press

[CORR] Calculates the correlation coefficient, 0.91.

[M] Calculates the slope coefficient, or the beta coefficient, 1.60.

[B] Calculates the Y-intercept, -8.92.

That's all there is to it!

Amortization

The amortization menu calculates the loan balance after payments are made and calculates the amount of the payments applied toward interest and principal.

Example:

Assume a $1,000 loan at 10 percent with annual payments is amortized over 3 years. Create an amortization schedule for this loan.

From the main menu, press [FIN] [TVM] [OTHER] [1] [P/YR] to set payments/year equal to 1.

Exit to the TVM menu and enter the following:

3 [N]

10 [I%YR]

1000 [PV]

Next, to calculate the payment press [PMT] and the loan payment of $402.11 is displayed.

Now press [OTHER] [AMRT] to enter the amortization menu.

Key in the number of payments for which to calculate the amortization schedule:

1 [#P] We entered 1 because we want to determine the principal paid, interest paid, and remaining balance after each payment is made.

Now press:

[INT] Displays interest paid in first year: "INTEREST = -100.0".

[PRIN] Displays principal paid in first year: "PRINCIPAL = -302.11".

[BAL] Displays balance at end of first year: "BALANCE = 697.89".

To calculate the amortization schedule for the second year, press [NEXT] [INT] [PRIN] [BAL].

Repeat for the third year.

The amortization table you create should contain these results. If not, try it again.

	Beg. Bal.	Payment	Interest	Princ. Repmt.	Ending Bal.
1	1,000.00	402.11	100.00	302.11	697.89
2	697.89	402.11	69.79	332.32	365.57
3	365.57	402.11	36.56	365.55	.02

Texas Instruments BAII PLUS Tutorial

To begin, look at the face of the calculator. Almost every key on the BAII PLUS has two functions: each key's primary function is noted on the key itself, while each key's secondary function is noted in white above the key. To use the function on the key, simply press the key. To access the white function above each key, first press the gray key with “2nd” printed on it, which we will call the "2nd shift" key, and then press the desired function key. (Note that the 2nd shift key is near the upper left corner of the calculator keyboard.)

Turning the Calculator On and Off

To turn on the calculator, press ON/OFF. To turn off the calculator, press ON/OFF.

Note that the “ON/OFF” key is on the upper right corner of the keyboard. Also, we will designate keys throughout this tutorial by the use of small boxes, as above. To conserve the battery, the calculator turns itself off about 10 minutes after your last keystroke.

Also, note that pressing the 2nd shift key places a little “2nd” symbol in the upper left corner of the display. Press the 2nd shift key again and the symbol goes away. The 2nd key is a toggle key that switches back and forth between the “regular” and the “2nd” functions. 2nd is like the typewriter shift key. After you press 2nd, look only at the white writing above the keys.

Note that the calculator has a continuous memory, so turning it off does not affect any data stored in the calculator, but it will erase any number showing on the screen.

Clearing the Calculator

Five of the most commonly used methods of clearing data are presented below:

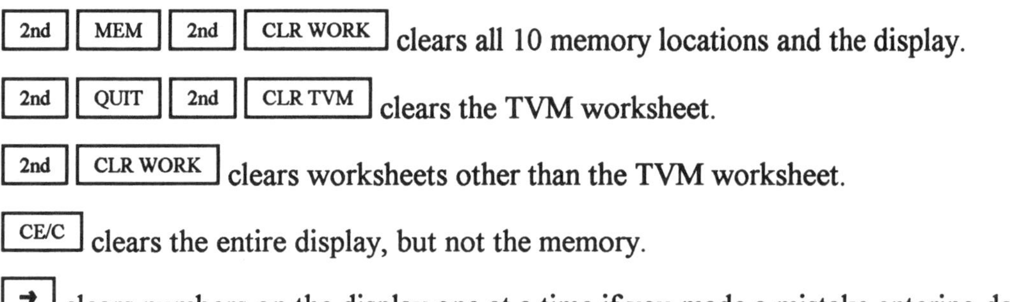

Review your owner’s manual for other methods of clearing information.

Clearing the calculator is very important, since unwanted data in memory can result in improper calculations, and hence wrong answers. It is best to get into the habit of automatically clearing memory before starting a calculation. Occasionally, you may purposely want to save data, but, in general, you will be entering all new data, so starting with a clear memory is the safest approach.

Changing the Display

To change decimals from 2 to 4, press [2nd] [FORMAT] [4] [ENTER] [2nd] [QUIT]. 0.0000 is displayed.

To change from 4 places to 2, press [2nd] [FORMAT] [2] [ENTER] [2nd] [QUIT]. 0.00 is displayed.

We usually set the display to 2 places, which is especially convenient when working with dollars and percentages. However, we often use 4 places when dealing with interest rates and rates of return that are entered as decimals.

Periods per Year Setting

One important setting that can cause problems is the periods per year setting. To check the current setting, press [2nd] [P/Y]. The display shows the setting for periods/year. The calculator comes pre-set at 12 periods per year, that is, it assumes calculations will be done on a monthly basis. However, finance textbook problems generally use 1 period/year. To change to 1/year:

Press [2nd] [P/Y] 1 [ENTER] [2nd] [QUIT].

Now the calculator is set to assume 1 period/year. To confirm this setting, press [2nd] [P/Y] [2nd] [QUIT]. Unless needed for other work, we generally leave the calculator setting at 1 period per year.

Time Value of Money (TVM)

The TVM keys are located on the third row from the top of the keyboard.

[N] [I/Y] [PV] [PMT] [FV]

In general, TVM problems involve four variables—three are known and the fourth is unknown.

Lump Sums

To begin, we consider TVM calculations with single (lump) sums. In this situation, we do not use the PMT key, so be sure to either press [2nd] [CLR TVM], which sets the payment (PMT) equal to 0, or enter 0 as the PMT when entering the input data. If you know any three variables, you can find the value of the fourth.

Example 1:

What is the FV of $100 after 3 years if the interest rate is 26 percent? First, clear with [2nd] [CLR TVM].

Next, enter the data.

3 [N]

26 [I/Y]

100 [PV]

0 [PMT] (Optional if registers are cleared.)

To determine the FV simply press [CPT] [FV] and the FV of -$200.04 is displayed.

The BAII PLUS is programmed so that if the PV is + then the FV is displayed as - and vice versa, because the BAII PLUS assumes that one is an inflow and the other is an outflow. When entering both PV and FV, one must be entered as negative and the other as positive.

Example 2:

What is the PV of $500 due in 5 years if the interest rate is 10 percent? Clear first and then enter the following data.

5 [N]

10 [I/Y]

0 [PMT] (Optional if registers are cleared.)

500 [FV]

Pressing the [CPT] [PV] key reveals that $310.46 will grow to $500 in 5 years at a 10 percent rate.

Example 3:

Assume a bond can be purchased today for $200. It will return $1,000 after 14 years. The bond pays no interest during its life. What rate of return would you earn if you bought the bond?

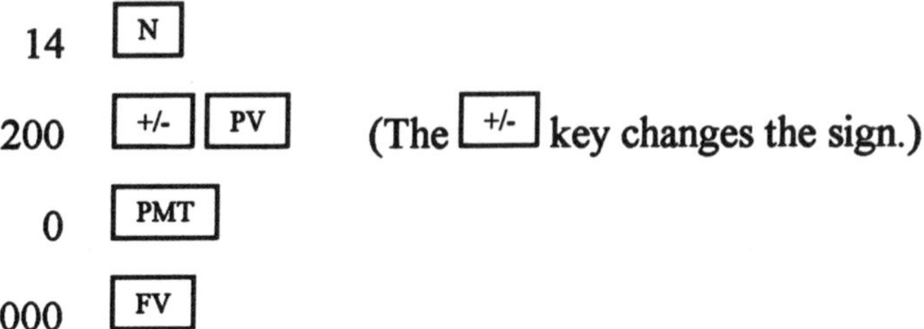

Simply press the CPT I/Y key and the BAII PLUS calculates the rate of return to be 12.18%.

Remember that the BAII PLUS is programmed so that if the PV is + then the FV is displayed as - and vice versa because the BAII PLUS assumes that one is an inflow and the other is an outflow.

Now suppose you learn that the bond will actually cost $300. What rate of return will you earn?

Override the -200 by entering 300 +/- PV, then press CPT I/Y to get 8.98 percent. If you pay more for the bond, you earn less on it. The important thing, though, is that you can do "what if" analyses with the calculator.

Now do nothing except press ON/OFF to turn off the calculator. Then turn on the calculator ON/OFF. The display shows 0.00. Is the memory erased? Not completely. What was on the screen is gone, but press RCL N to get N = 14.

Ordinary Annuities

Example 1:

What is the FV of an annuity of $100 paid at the end of each year for 5 years if the interest rate equals 6 percent?

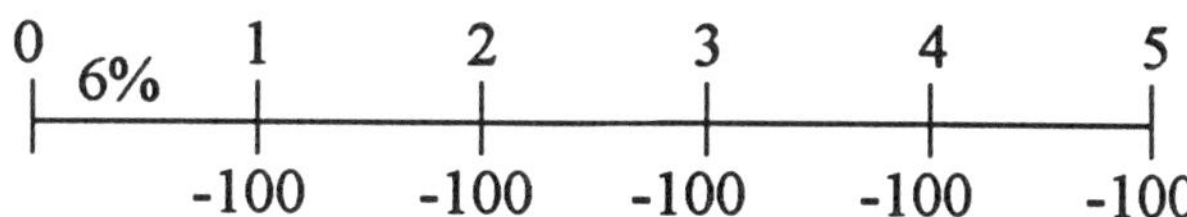

5 [N]

6 [I/Y]

0 [PV]

100 [+/-] [PMT]

Now press the [CPT] [FV] key, and an FV of $563.71 is displayed.

Example 2:

What is the PV of the same annuity?

Leave data in calculator, but enter 0 as the FV to override, then press [CPT] [PV] to get $421.24.

Annuities Due

Each payment of an annuity due occurs at the beginning of the period instead of at the end as with a regular annuity. In essence, each payment is shifted back one period. To analyze annuities due press [2nd] [BGN] [2nd] [SET] [CE/C]. "BGN" appears on the screen and in the upper right corner of the display. Now the BAII PLUS analyzes the cash flows based on beginning of period payments. Change back to end mode by pressing [2nd] [BGN] [2nd] [SET] [CE/C].

Interest Conversion

The following equation is used to convert a nominal rate to an effective rate.

$$\text{EAR} = \left[1 + \frac{k_{\text{Nom}}}{m}\right]^m - 1.$$

Given: $k_{\text{Nom}} = 10\%$ and m = 12 payments/year,

$$\text{EAR} = \left[1 + \frac{0.10}{12}\right]^m - 1 = (1.0083)^{12} - 1 = 1.1047 - 1 = 0.1047 = 10.47\%.$$

However, it's much easier to convert the nominal rate using the calculator.

First, we need to set the calculator to 12 payments per year:

[2nd] [I CONV] [↑] 12 [ENTER]

[↓] 10 [ENTER]

[↓] [CPT]

The effective rate of 10.47 percent is displayed on the screen.

Cash Flow Operations

Example 1: Uneven Cash Flows

We can also find the PV, FV, and IRR (internal rate of return) of a series of unequal cash flows.

Assume the following cash flows:

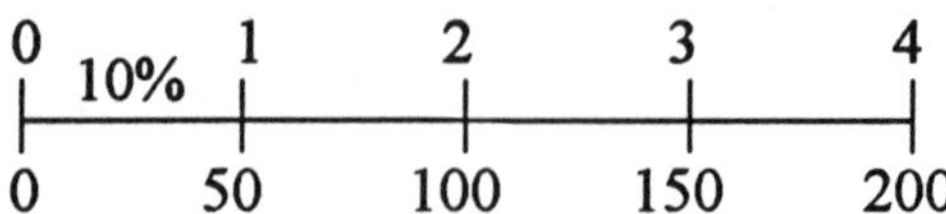

What is the PV of these CFs?

First clear the BAII PLUS and make sure that periods/year is set equal to 1.

Enter the cash flow worksheet by pressing [CF] then clear any previous cash flow analyses, [2nd] [CLR WORK]. Next, enter the cash flows:

0	[ENTER] [↓]	Sets CF_0 equal to 0 and moves to CF_1.
50	[ENTER] [↓]	Sets CF_1 equal to 50 and moves to frequency of occurrence of CF_1.
1	[ENTER] [↓]	Tells calculator that the \$50 CF occurs only once.
100	[ENTER] [↓]	
1	[ENTER] [↓]	
150	[ENTER] [↓]	
1	[ENTER] [↓]	
200	[ENTER] [↓]	
1	[ENTER]	

The CFs from the time line are entered. Now enter the interest rate.

[NPV] 10 [ENTER] [↓]

At this point the BAII PLUS knows the cash flows, the number of periods, and the interest rate. To find the PV, press [CPT] to get PV = NPV = \$377.40.

Example 2: Embedded Annuities

We have these cash flows, which contain embedded annuities:

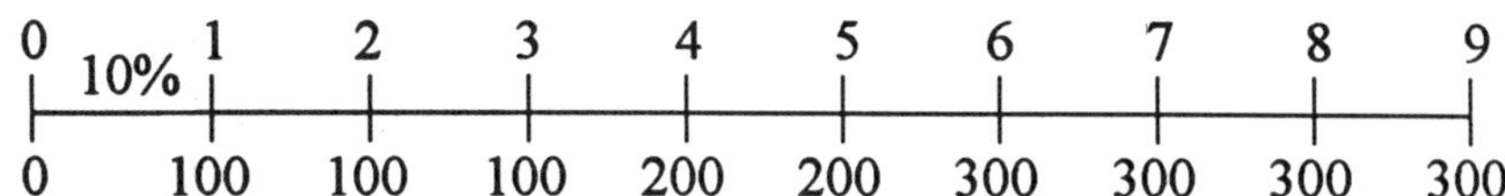

What's the PV?

Clear, set P/YR = 1 if changed.

First enter the cash flow worksheet by pressing [CF] then clear any previous cash flow analyses, [2nd] [CLR WORK]. Next, enter the cash flows:

0	[ENTER] [↓]	Sets CF_0 equal to 0 and moves to CF_1.
100	[ENTER] [↓]	Sets CF_1 equal to 100 and moves to frequency of occurrence of CF_1.
3	[ENTER] [↓]	Tells calculator that the $100 CF occurs three consecutive times.
200	[ENTER] [↓]	
2	[ENTER] [↓]	
300	[ENTER] [↓]	
4	[ENTER]	

Now the BAII PLUS knows the cash flows. Thus, enter the interest rate:

[NPV] 10 [ENTER] [↓].

At this point the BAII PLUS knows the cash flows, the number of periods, and the interest rate. To find the PV, press [CPT] to get PV = NPV = $1,099.94.

To check your entries:

[CF] then use the up and down arrow keys to view each cash flow.

Example 3: The Rate of Return Offered by an Investment (IRR)[1]

Assume that we invest $1,000 now (t = 0) and then expect to receive an uneven set of cash flows. Here is the CF time line:

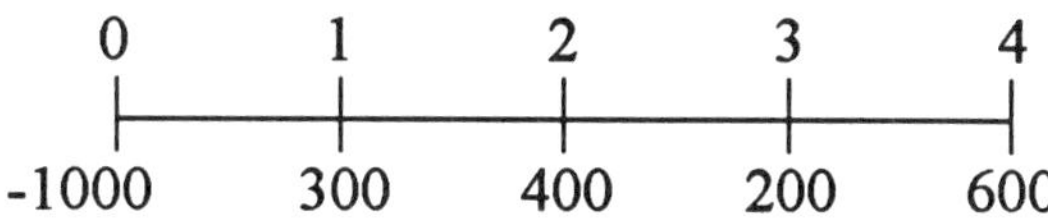

What rate of return will we earn?

First enter the cash flow worksheet by pressing [CF] then clear any previous cash flow analyses, [2nd] [CLR WORK]. Next, enter the cash flows:

1000	[+/-] [ENTER] [↓]	Sets CF_0 equal to -1,000 and moves to CF_1.
300	[ENTER] [↓] [↓]	Sets CF_1 equal to -1000 and moves to frequency of occurrence of CF_1. The second [↓] tells calculator that the $300 CF occurs only once.[2]
400	[ENTER] [↓] [↓]	
200	[ENTER] [↓] [↓]	
600	[ENTER] [↓] [↓]	

Now the BAII PLUS knows the cash flows. Thus, simply press [IRR] [CPT] and the IRR of 16.71 percent is displayed.

---

[1]If a negative CF occurs at the end of a project's life, or if a sequence of cash flows has two or more sign changes, there may be multiple IRR solutions. The calculator displays the IRR closest to zero. However, the displayed solution has no financial meaning. Thus, you should use caution in making investment decisions based on an IRR computed for a cash flow stream with more than one sign change. When you are solving very complex cash flow problems, the calculator may not be able to find IRR, even if a solution exists. When this is the case, the calculator displays *Error 7* (iteration limit exceeded).

[2]If you do not enter a value for frequency after you enter the cash flow value, the calculator assumes a value of 1; however, the down arrow key must be pressed again before entering the next cash flow.

You can also determine the NPV of the investment. Leave data entered and then enter the opportunity cost interest rate, say 8 percent. To find NPV press

[I/YR] 8 [ENTER] [↓] [CPT]

The NPV of $220.50 is displayed. Thus, the PV of the cash inflows exceeds the cost of the investment by $220.50.

Statistical Calculations

The BAII PLUS can also be used for several types of statistical calculations.

Mean and Standard Deviation (σ)

Year	Sales
1994	$150
1995	95
1996	260

What's the mean (average) and standard deviation (σ) of sales over the 3 years?

First select the data-entry portion of the statistics worksheet by pressing [2nd] [DATA] then clear any previous data entries, [2nd] [CLR WORK]. Next, enter the data:

150 [ENTER] [↓] [↓] — This enters 150 as the data entry and tells the calculator there is no Y-variable associated with the X variable.

95 [ENTER] [↓] [↓] — This enters 95 as the second data entry and tells the calculator there is no Y-variable associated with the X variable.

260 [ENTER] [↓] [↓] — This enters 260 as the third data entry and tells the calculator there is no Y-variable associated with the X variable.

Now select the statistical calculation portion of the statistics worksheet by pressing [2nd] [STAT] then clear any previous statistical entries, [2nd] [CLR WORK].

"LIN" should now be displayed on the screen. Keep pressing [2nd] then [SET] until "1-V" (one variable calculation method) is displayed. Press the down arrow key three times to view (1) sample size, n, (2) mean, $\overline{x}$, and (3) standard deviation, Sx. The mean equals $168.33. The standard deviation is $84.01.

Linear Regression

Beta coefficients can be calculated by using the BAII PLUS's linear regression capabilities. The X (independent variable) and Y (dependent variable) values must be entered in the proper sequence, where the X data is on the horizontal axis (**market**) and Y data is on the vertical axis (**stock**).

Year	Market (k_m)	Stock (k_j)
1	23.8%	38.6%
2	-7.2	-24.7
3	6.6	12.3
4	20.5	8.2
5	30.6	40.1

First select the data-entry portion of the statistics worksheet by pressing [2nd] [DATA] then clear any previous statistical entries, [2nd] [CLR WORK].

Next, enter the data as follows:

23.8	[ENTER] [↓]	This enters 23.8 as the first X variable.
38.6	[ENTER] [↓]	This enters 38.6 as the first Y variable.
7.2	[+/-] [ENTER] [↓]	This enters -7.2 as the second X variable.
24.7	[+/-] [ENTER] [↓]	This enters -24.7 as the second Y variable.
6.6	[ENTER] [↓]	This enters 6.6 as the third X variable.
12.3	[ENTER] [↓]	This enters 12.3 as the third Y variable.
20.5	[ENTER] [↓]	This enters 20.5 as the fourth X variable.
8.2	[ENTER] [↓]	This enters 8.2 as the fourth Y variable.
30.6	[ENTER] [↓]	This enters 30.6 as the fifth X variable.
40.1	[ENTER] [↓]	This enters 40.1 as the fifth Y variable.

Now select the statistical calculation portion of the statistics worksheet by pressing [2nd] [STAT] then clear any previous statistical entries, [2nd] [CLR WORK].

"LIN" should now be displayed on the screen. Keep pressing [↓] until "a =" appears on the screen. This is the value of the y-intercept of the regression line. Press [↓] one more time and "b =" appears one the screen. This is the value of the slope of the regression line. If you press [↓] one more time, "r =" appears on the screen. This is the value of the correlation coefficient of the regression line. (The intercept value is -8.92, the slope value is 1.60, and the correlation coefficient is 0.91.)

Clear the calculator by pressing [2nd] [DATA] [2nd] [CLR WORK].

Amortization

The BAII PLUS can also be used to calculate amortization schedules. First, clear the TVM registers by pressing [2nd] [QUIT] [2nd] [CLR TVM].

Example:

Determine the interest and principal paid each year and the balance at the end of each year on a three-year $1,000 amortizing loan which carries an interest rate of 10 percent. The payments are due annually.

First, check payments/year and be sure it's 1. ([2nd] [P/Y] [2nd] [QUIT])

Now perform the following steps:

3 [N]

10 [I/Y]

1000 [PV]

[CPT] [PMT] A payment of -402.11 is displayed.

Now we will use the amortization worksheet to generate an amortization schedule for the loan:

[2nd] [AMORT] [2nd] [CLR WORK] — Enters the Amort worksheet and clears any old contents.

[↓] 1 [ENTER] — Ending period set at 1 because we want to view the amortization information for each and every payment.

Now just use the down arrow key to view the balance after the payment as well as the interest and principal portions of the first payment.

To view the results for the second payment, press [↓] to move to "P1," press [CPT] and use the down arrow key to view the ending balance after the payment is made as well as the interest and principal portions of the second payment.

Repeat for the third and last payment.

This is the amortization schedule corresponding to the loan.

	Beg. Bal.	Payment	Interest	Princ. Repmt.	Ending Bal.
1	1,000.00	402.11	100.00	302.11	697.89
2	697.89	402.11	69.79	332.32	365.57
3	365.57	402.11	36.56	365.55	.02

Sharp EL-733A Tutorial

To begin, look at the face of the calculator. Almost every key on the EL-733A has two functions: each key's primary function is noted on the key itself, while each key's secondary function is noted in reddish-brown above the key. To use the function on the key, simply press the key. To access the function above each key, first press the yellow key with "2ndF" printed on it, which we will call the "2nd function" key, and then press the desired function key. (Note that the 2nd function key is located at the upper left corner of the calculator keyboard.)

Turning the Calculator On and Off

To turn on the calculator, press [C-CE]. To turn off the calculator, press [OFF].

Note that the ON and OFF keys are in the upper right corner of the keyboard. Also, we will designate keys throughout this tutorial by the use of small boxes, as above. To conserve the battery, the calculator turns itself off about 10 minutes after your last keystroke.

Also, note that pressing the 2nd function key places a little "2ndF" symbol in the upper left corner of the display. Press the 2nd function key again and the symbol goes away. The [2ndF] key is a toggle key that switches back and forth between the "regular" and the "2nd" functions. [2ndF] is like the typewriter shift key. After you press [2ndF], look only at the reddish-brown writing above the keys.

Note that the calculator has a continuous memory, so turning it off does not affect any data stored in the calculator, but will erase any number showing on the screen.

Clearing the Calculator

Three of the most commonly used methods of clearing data are presented below:

[2ndF] [CA]	Clears all the memory registers associated with a particular mode (normal, FIN, or STAT).
[C-CE]	Clears the entire display, but not the memory.
[→]	Clears numbers on the display one at a time if you made a mistake entering data.

Review your owner's manual for other methods of clearing information.

Clearing the calculator is very important, since unwanted data in memory can result in improper calculations, and hence wrong answers. It is best to get into the habit of automatically clearing memory before starting a calculation. Occasionally, you may purposely want to save data, but, in general, you will be entering all new data, so starting with a clear memory is the safest approach.

Changing the Display

To change decimals from 2 to 4, press [2ndF] [TAB] [4]. 0.0000 is displayed.

To change from 4 places to 2, press [2ndF] [TAB] [2]. 0.00 is displayed.

We usually set the display to 2 places, which is especially convenient when working with dollars and percentages. However, we often use 4 places when dealing with interest rates and rates of return that are entered as decimals.

Changing the Mode

The calculator has three calculation modes: NORMAL, FIN (financial), and STAT (statistics). The mode of the calculator dictates the type of calculations that can be performed. When working financial problems, you will typically use the FIN mode, while statistical problems normally will be handled in STAT mode. Modes are indicated in the display as follows: a box showing "FIN" indicates finance mode, a box showing "STAT" indicates statistics mode, and no box appears when in the normal mode. To change modes, simply press, [2ndF] [MODE]. The calculator rotates through the modes from normal to finance to statistics to normal.

Time Value of Money (TVM)

The TVM keys are located on the third row from the top of the keyboard.

[n] [i] [PV] [FV] [PMT]

To enter the time value of money mode do the following:

Press [2ndF] [MODE] repeatedly until the [FIN] indicator appears in the display.

In general, TVM problems involve four variables—three are known and the fourth is unknown.

Lump Sums

To begin, we consider TVM calculations with single (lump) sums. In this situation, we do not use the PMT key, so be sure to either clear all, which sets the payment (PMT) equal to 0, or enter 0 as the PMT when entering the input data. If you know any three variables, you can find the value of the fourth.

Example 1:

What is the FV of $100 after 3 years if the interest rate is 26 percent? First, clear with [2ndF] [CA].

Next, enter the data.

3 [n]

26 [i]

100 [PV]

0 [PMT] (Optional if registers are cleared.)

To determine the FV simply press [COMP] [FV] and the FV of -$200.04 is displayed. (COMP is the key framed in black near the upper left corner.)

The EL-733A is programmed so that if the PV is + then the FV is displayed as - and vice versa, because the EL-733A assumes that one is an inflow and the other is an outflow. When entering both PV and FV, one must be entered as negative and the other as positive.

Example 2:

What is the PV of $500 due in 5 years if the interest rate is 10 percent? Clear first and then enter the following data.

5 [n]

10 [i]

0 [PMT] (Optional if registers are cleared.)

500 [FV]

Pressing the [COMP] [PV] key reveals that $310.46 will grow to $500 in 5 years at a 10 percent rate.

Example 3:

Assume a bond can be purchased today for $200. It will return $1,000 after 14 years. The bond pays no interest during its life. What rate of return would you earn if you bought the bond?

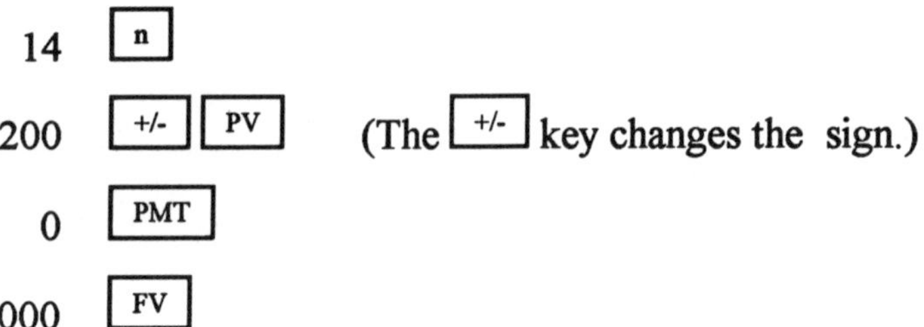

Simply press the COMP i key and the HP calculates the rate of return to be 12.18%.

Remember that the EL-733A is programmed so that if the PV is + then the FV is displayed as - and vice versa, because the EL-733A assumes that one is an inflow and other is an outflow. Also, note that the negative sign is placed on the 200 PV entry by pressing the key marked "+/-".

Now suppose you learn that the bond will actually cost $300. What rate of return will you earn?

Override the -200 by entering 300 +/- PV, then press COMP i to get 8.98 percent. If you pay more for the bond, you earn less on it. The important thing, though, is that you can do "what if" analyses with the calculator.

Now do nothing except press OFF to turn off the calculator. Then turn on the calculator C-CE. The display shows 0.00. Is the memory erased? Not completely. What was on the screen is gone, but press 2ndF RCL n to see that the N = 14 entry is still in the calculator's memory.

Ordinary Annuities

Example 1:

What is the FV of an annuity of $100 paid at the end of each year for 5 years if the interest rate equals 6 percent?

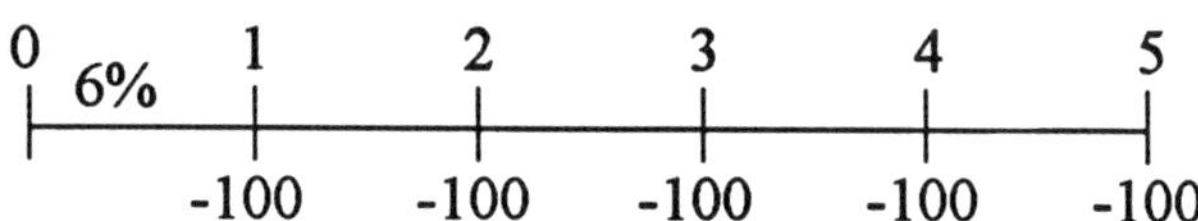

5 [n]

6 [i]

0 [PV]

100 [+/-] [PMT]

Now press the [COMP] [FV] key, and an FV of $563.71 is displayed.

Example 2:

What is the PV of the same annuity?

Leave data in calculator, but enter 0 as the FV to override, then press [COMP] [PV] to get $421.24.

Annuities Due

Each payment of an annuity due occurs at the beginning of the period instead of at the end as with a regular annuity. In essence, each payment is shifted back one period. To analyze annuities due press [BGN]. The symbol "BGN" appears in the upper right corner of the display. Now the EL-733A analyzes the cash flows based on beginning of period payments. Change back to end mode by pressing [BGN] again.

Interest Conversion

The following equation is used to convert a nominal rate to an effective rate.

$$EAR = \left[1 + \frac{k_{Nom}}{m}\right]^m - 1.$$

Given: $k_{Nom} = 10\%$ and $m = 12$ payments/year,

$$EAR = \left[1 + \frac{0.10}{12}\right]^m - 1 = (1.0083)^{12} - 1 = 1.1047 - 1 = 0.1047 = 10.47\%.$$

However, it's much easier to convert the nominal rate using the calculator.

Before beginning this procedure it is important to note that another name for the nominal rate is the annual percentage rate (APR). In fact, the EL-733A uses the term APR for the nominal interest rate. Thus, the keystrokes required to calculate the above effective rate for 12 compounding periods would be as follows:

12 [2ndF] [→EFF] 10 [=]

The effective rate of 10.47% is displayed on the screen.

If you were given the effective rate and wished to convert it to an APR (nominal rate), the key strokes for 12 compounding periods would be as follows:

12 [2ndF] [→APR] 10.4713 [=]

The nominal rate of 10.00 percent is displayed on the screen.

Cash Flow Operations

We can also find the PV, FV, and IRR (internal rate of return) of a series of unequal cash flows.

Example 1: Uneven Cash Flows

Assume the following cash flows:

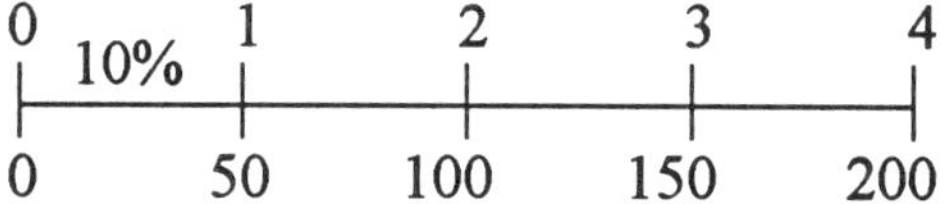

What is the PV of these CFs?

First clear any previous cash flow or TVM analyses by pressing [2ndF] [CA]. Next, enter the cash flows:

0 [CF*i*] Sets CF_0 equal to 0 and moves to CF_1.

50 [CF*i*] Sets CF_1 equal to 50 and so on.

100 [CF*i*]

150 [CF*i*]

200 [CF*i*]

The CFs from the time line are entered. Now enter the interest rate.

10 [i]

At this point the EL-733A knows the cash flows, the number of periods, and the interest rate. To find the PV, press [COMP] [NPV] to get PV = NPV = $377.40.

Example 2: Embedded Annuities

We have these cash flows, which contain embedded annuities:

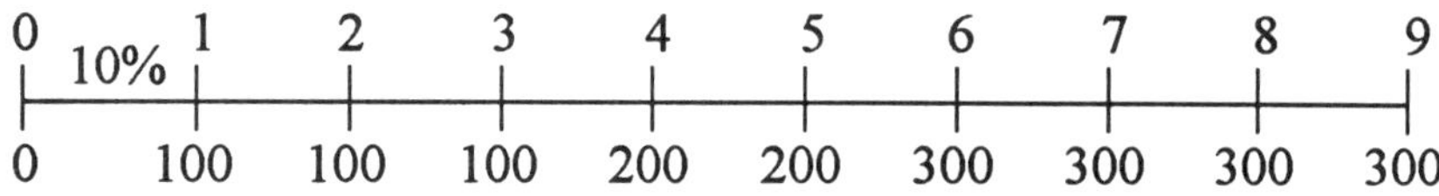

What's the PV?

First clear any previous cash flow analyses, [2ndF] [CA]. Next, enter the cash flows:

0	[CF*i*]	Sets CF_0 equal to 0 and moves to CF_1.
3	[2ndF] [N*i*]	Tells the calculator that the *following* CF will occur three consecutive times.
100	[CF*i*]	Sets the first three CFs equal to 100.
2	[2ndF] [N*i*]	
200	[CF*i*]	
4	[2ndF] [N*i*]	
300	[CF*i*]	

Now the EL-733A knows the cash flows. Thus, enter the interest rate:

10 [i]

At this point the EL-733A knows the cash flows, the number of periods, and the interest rate. To find the PV, press [COMP] [NPV] to get PV = NPV = $1,099.94.

To check your entries:

Press [2ndF] [RCL] [1] to see that the amount of the first group of CFs is $100.00 each. You can now check the frequency of this CF group by pressing [2ndF] [RCL] [2ndF] [N*i*]. This $100.00 cash flow occurs 3 consecutive times.

Example 3: The Rate of Return Offered by an Investment (IRR)[1]

Assume that we invest $1,000 now (t = 0) and then expect to receive an uneven set of cash flows. Here is the CF time line:

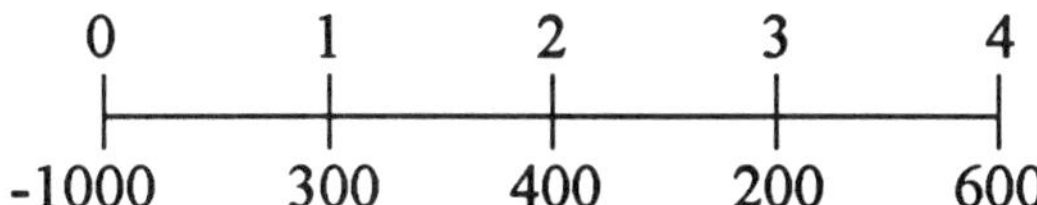

What rate of return will we earn?

First clear any previous cash flow analyses, [2ndF] [CA]. Next, enter the cash flows:

1000	[+/-] [CF*i*]	Sets CF_0 equal to -1000 and moves to CF_1.
300	[CF*i*]	Sets CF_1 equal to 300 and moves to CF_2.
400	[CF*i*]	
200	[CF*i*]	
600	[CF*i*]	

Now the EL-733A knows the cash flows. Thus, simply press [COMP] [IRR] and the IRR of 16.71 percent is displayed.

You can also determine the NPV of the investment. Leave data entered and then enter the opportunity cost interest rate, say 8 percent. To find NPV press

8 [i] [COMP] [NPV]

The NPV of $220.50 is displayed. Thus, the PV of the cash inflows exceeds the cost of the investment by $220.50.

---

[1]If a negative CF occurs at the end of a project's life, or if a sequence of cash flows has two or more sign changes, there may be multiple IRR solutions. The calculator displays the IRR closest to zero. However, the displayed solution has no financial meaning. Thus, you should use caution in making investment decisions based on an IRR computed for a cash flow stream with more than one sign change. When you are solving very complex cash flow problems, the calculator may not be able to find IRR, even if a solution exists. When this is the case, the calculator displays *E*. An error can be cleared by pressing the [C-CE] key.

Statistical Calculations

The EL-733A can also be used for several types of statistical calculations.

Mean and Standard Deviation (σ)

Year	Sales
1994	$150
1995	95
1996	260

What's the mean (average) and standard deviation (σ) of sales over the 3 years?

First, put the calculator into the Statistics mode by pressing [2ndF] [MODE] until the [STAT] indicator shows on the display. Then clear any previous data entries, [2ndF] [CA]. Next, enter the data:

150 [M+]	This enters 150 as the data entry and tells the calculator it occurs one time. Note that [DATA] is the meaning of the [M+] key when the calculator is in the statistics (STAT) mode.
95 [M+]	This enters 95 as the second data entry and tells the calculator it occurs one time.
260 [M+]	This enters 260 as the third data entry and tells the calculator it occurs one time.

Determine the mean by simply pressing the following:

[2ndF] [$\overline{X}$] The mean equals $168.33.

Determine the standard deviation by pressing the following:

[2ndF] [S_x] The standard deviation is $84.01. S_x and S_y are sample standard deviations. σ_x and σ_y refer to population statistics.

Linear Regression

Beta coefficients can be calculated by using the EL-733A's linear regression capabilities. The X (independent variable) and Y (dependent variable) values must be entered in the proper sequence, where the X data is on the horizontal axis (**market**) and Y data is on the vertical axis (**stock**).

Year	Market (k_m)	Stock (k_j)
1	23.8%	38.6%
2	-7.2	-24.7
3	6.6	12.3
4	20.5	8.2
5	30.6	40.1

First, put the calculator into the Statistics mode by pressing [2ndF] [MODE] until the [STAT] indicator shows on the display. The clear any previous data entries, [2ndF] [CA]. Next, enter the data as follows:

23.8	[RM]	This enters 23.8 as the first X variable. (The [RM] key in the STAT mode is the [(x, y)] key.)
38.6	[M+]	This enters 38.6 as the first Y variable.
7.2	[+/-] [RM]	This enters -7.2 as the second X variable.
24.7	[+/-] [M+]	This enters -24.7 as the second Y variable.
6.6	[RM]	This enters 6.6 as the third X variable.
12.3	[M+]	This enters 12.3 as the third Y variable.
20.5	[RM]	This enters 20.5 as the fourth X variable.
8.2	[M+]	This enters 8.2 as the fourth Y variable.
30.6	[RM]	This enters 30.6 as the fifth X variable.
40.1	[M+]	This enters 4.1 as the fifth Y variable.

Determine the intercept by pressing [2ndF] [a]. The display shows that "a," which is the *vertical axis intercept*, is equal to -8.92. To find the slope simply press [2ndF] [b]. The display shows that "b" is equal to 1.60, which is the slope coefficient and the *beta coefficient*.

Amortization

The EL-733A can also be used to calculate amortization schedules.

Example:

Determine the interest and principal paid each year and the balance at the end of each year on a three-year $1,000 amortizing loan which carries an interest rate of 10 percent. The payments are due annually.

Press [2ndF] [MODE] repeatedly until the [FIN] indicator comes on the display screen. Then clear any previous data entries, [2ndF] [CA].

Now perform the following steps:

3 [n]

10 [i]

1000 [PV]

[COMP] [PMT] A payment of -$402.11 is displayed.

Now, since all the information about the loan is stored in the TVM register, we can use the amortization functions to generate an amortization schedule for the loan.

Determine the principal and interest paid in each payment, and the balance remaining after each payment by doing the following steps:

1	AMRT	Entering 1 tells the calculator we want to examine the first year. The display shows that PRN = -302.11. Thus, out of the first $402.11 payment, $302.11 went toward paying off the principal portion of the loan.
	AMRT	The display shows that INT = -100.00. Thus, out of the first $402.11 payment, $100.00 was payment of interest.
	AMRT	The display shows that BAL = 697.89. Thus, after making the first $402.11 payment, the principal balance you to be paid is $697.89.
2	AMRT	The 2 moves to the second year. The display shows that the principal repayment is Year 2 is PRN = -332.33.
	AMRT	The interest payment is INT = -69.79.
	AMRT	The remaining balance is BAL = 365.56.
3	AMRT	For Year 3, the principal repayment is PRN = -365.56.
	AMRT	The interest payment is INT = -36.56.
	AMRT	The remaining balance is BAL = 0.

Here is the complete amortization table:

	Beg. Bal.	Payment	Interest	Princ. Repmt.	Ending Bal.
1	1,000.00	402.11	100.00	302.11	697.89
2	697.89	402.11	69.79	332.33	365.56
3	365.56	402.11	36.56	365.56	0.00

Spreadsheet Tutorial

By

Laura A. Eakins[1] and Stanley G. Eakins[2]
East Carolina University

[1] Department of Decision Sciences
[2] Department of Finance

INTRODUCTION

The Information Age is upon us. In 1957, for the first time in history, white collar workers outnumbered blue collar workers, signaling the beginning of a new era, a period where information would rule supreme. More jobs now deal with the gathering, processing, and disseminating of information than ever before. Along with this new age came rapid advancements in computer hardware and software and, therefore, tremendous changes in financial management. Microcomputers more powerful than mainframes of a few years ago are now affordable to any business, and new and improved software makes it easy to do things that were not feasible several years ago.

Because so many businesses rely on computers, it is crucial that anyone with a serious interest in financial management develop at least a minimal level of spreadsheet literacy. Most employers realize that students with solid computer skills are a valuable asset to any business. Today, students who are not comfortable with microcomputers, spreadsheets, word processing, and inter-computer communications are not very marketable.

The first electronic spreadsheet program was called Visicalc (short for visible calculator) and was developed in 1979 by two students at Harvard University. The program was written to run on an Apple II personal computer. Because it was the first of its kind, this program caused widespread interest in the new and growing world of personal computers. It is estimated that Visicalc alone was responsible for the sale of over 20,000 Apple computers.

Since the days of Visicalc, many computer programs such as Excel, Lotus 1-2-3, and QuattroPro have been developed for working with spreadsheets. A spreadsheet is simply a tool used for quantitative analysis. An electronic spreadsheet program is the computerized equivalent of the old manual system of recording information on a ledger sheet. The purpose is to record data in a logical, organized manner.

A spreadsheet consists of a grid or matrix of rows and columns. The intersection of a row and a column forms a cell which can hold numbers, text, or a formula. The spreadsheet's usefulness comes from its ability to recalculate results as you change the contents of other cells. The user need not do these calculations by hand or on a calculator anymore. Rather, an electronic spreadsheet should be used with formulas inserted into some cells. In this way, the spreadsheet recalculates the desired values automatically. Every time the content of a cell changes, any formulas relating to that cell are automatically recalculated.

In these instances, the spreadsheet is set up to perform "what if" analysis. What if sales are below the expected level? What if costs of manufacturing go up? With a properly constructed spreadsheet using formulas, any data changes will result in a recalculation of the spreadsheet, and the impact of the change on net income is shown immediately. For this reason, spreadsheets are used extensively in financial planning and analysis, instances that involve large amounts of numerical data.

GETTING STARTED

In this tutorial, basic information will be presented on using spreadsheets. The tutorial is based on Microsoft Excel, version 7.0. Where applicable, guidelines will also be noted for using Lotus 1-2-3 for Windows, version 5.0. These guidelines will be inserted in the form of "Lotus Tip" boxes. By comparing the two programs, you will find that they are remarkably similar since both are Windows based. We will only note significant differences between the two. If a Lotus Tip does not appear in the text, assume that Excel and Lotus function in a similar manner.

Before you can do any work with your spreadsheet, you have to load the program into your computer's memory. The location of the Excel or Lotus icon will depend on the organization of your system. In Windows 3.1, if you are using Program Manager as the main shell, locate the Excel or Lotus icon and double click on that icon. In Windows95 click on the Start button in the bottom left corner of your screen, then choose **P**rograms and then Microsoft Excel or Lotus 1-2-3.

Lotus Tip

In Lotus the program will present a dialog box asking whether you wish to open a new spreadsheet or work on an existing spreadsheet. If you choose to work on an existing sheet, the program then loads that sheet for you. If you choose to start a new spreadsheet, you are presented with another dialog box that offers you a choice of several worksheet templates. Press the enter key if you wish to accept the default Lotus setting, which opens a plain worksheet.

IDENTIFYING PARTS OF THE WORKSHEET

The following page shows the Excel screen as it will first appear when you enter the program. The various parts of the screen have been identified. We will discuss each part in detail in the sections that follow.

Lotus Tip

The appendix shows the Lotus screen. Lotus looks slightly different from Excel. These differences will be noted in the appendix.

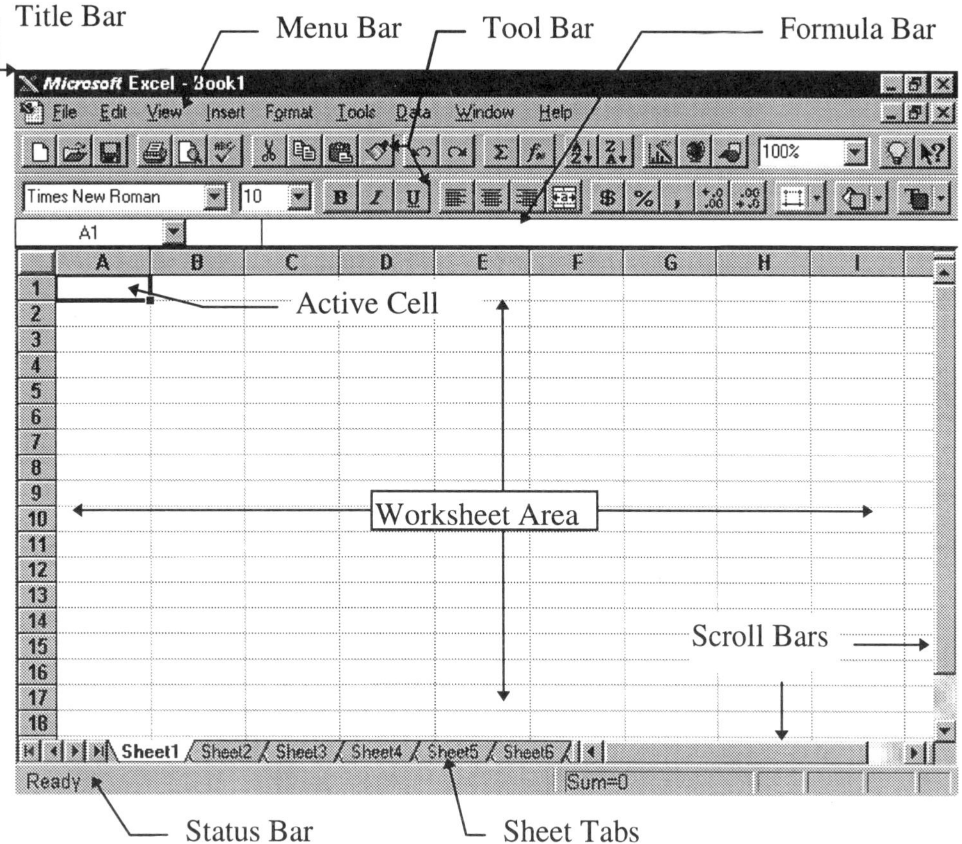

The Title Bar

Microsoft Excel - Book1

The title bar is located at the top of the Excel screen. In the far left corner of the title bar is the application control button, which in Excel 7.0 looks like an "X," short for Excel. Clicking once on this button causes a menu to drop down that controls the application window. This menu allows choices for moving the window, changing its size, and closing the program, as well as the ability to switch to or run other programs. Clicking twice on this button closes the program. To the right of the application control button is the name of the program and the workbook that is currently active.

The right side of the title bar has three buttons. From left to right, the first button is the minimize button. It will reduce the window down to a box on the taskbar at the bottom of the Windows screen where it is still active, but out of the way. The second button is the restore button. Clicking on it will restore the window back to a smaller window that does not occupy the whole screen. This allows the Windows desktop screen to be visible also. Once you have clicked on the restore button, this new smaller window has the maximize button as the second button instead of the restore button. The maximize button expands the window, causing it to occupy the entire screen again. The third button looks like an "X" and closes the program.

The Menu Bar

The main menu bar in Excel is located directly under the title bar. On the far left side of the menu bar is the document control button, which looks like a small "x" on top of a document. Clicking once on this button causes the same menu to drop down that is present when you click on the application control button above it. Clicking twice on this button closes the worksheet. The remainder of the menu bar allows access to the nine menus available in the program. Choosing one of these menu items leads you to the options that are available under that particular item. There are two ways to select a menu: click on the menu of choice with the mouse, or use the Alt key in combination with the underlined letter in the menu name. For example, to choose the File menu, either click with the mouse on the word "File" or press Alt-F on the keyboard. Either method will lead to the File menu dropping down, allowing you to make another choice.

Notice that when you are working in the Windows program, menus stay visible on the screen until you either make a selection or cancel the menu by pressing the Esc key or clicking the mouse anywhere outside the menu. These menus are said to be persistent, meaning they remain on the screen. While the menu is visible, using the arrow keys or the mouse to highlight individual menu choices will cause a short help message to be displayed at the bottom of the Excel screen. This help message describes what action the highlighted menu selection performs. Memorization of the menus is really not necessary. By simply scrolling through the menus in this manner, you will eventually learn where items are located. Once you locate the option that you want to select, simply click the left mouse button or press Enter.

Sometimes when you choose a menu, some of the selections in the drop down menu beneath it will be displayed in a light gray color instead of black. This means that these options are not available for selection at this time. For example, if you have not cut or copied a cell, the Paste option from the Edit menu has nothing to paste, so it is grayed indicating that it is not available as an option at this time. Once you have cut or copied some data, the paste function will be shown in black type, indicating that the option is available to you to use. Remember, only the menu options displayed in black may be selected.

Some menu selections will be followed by a series of three periods. This indicates that once that menu item is selected, a dialog box will appear and more information will be needed. For example, if you select the Print option from the File menu, the program will need more information from you as to what part of the spreadsheet you want to print, how many copies, and so forth. When a menu selection is not followed by three periods, it means that selecting that option will carry out the task and no dialog box will appear.

The last item on the menu bar is the "Help" option. The Help Menu can guide you through the steps necessary to accomplish any task using Microsoft Excel. For example, suppose you don't know how to put a border around text in your spreadsheet. Choose Help, Microsoft

Excel Help Topics, then choose Index and type the word "border" in the box provided. From there, the program will instruct you on how to add a border to your spreadsheet. The Help Menu can be a valuable tool when using a spreadsheet program. It is worth your time to become familiar with using the Help option since the Excel user manual is very abbreviated. Lotus does not even include a manual with its program when it is packaged on CD-Rom.

The Toolbar

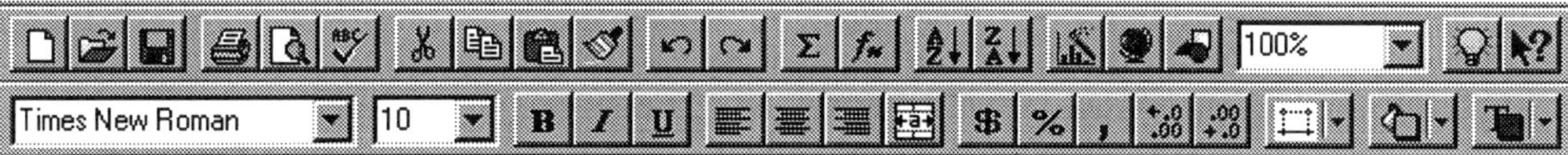

The toolbar is located directly below the menu bar on the Excel screen. It displays a series of buttons with pictures or icons that represent short-cuts. These buttons provide a quick way to carry out certain commands that are used frequently in Excel without wading through menus and dialog boxes. The exact buttons and their order may be different on different computers. This is because the Excel program can be customized to meet your particular needs. To add, delete, or rearrange buttons choose View Toolbars from the menus.

To learn what function each button performs, simply move the mouse pointer over the button. Almost immediately a box will appear directly under the mouse pointer that lists the button's function. Also, at the bottom of the Excel screen, a more detailed description of the button's function will appear.

The Formula Bar

The formula bar has three separate sections. The left part of the formula bar is called the reference area since it indicates the name of the active cell. The center section remains blank until you begin to type an entry into a cell. As soon as the first keystroke is made, three symbols appear in this section. By clicking on the first symbol, an "X," you cancel the entry you were going to put into the cell. Clicking on the second symbol, a check mark, enters what you have typed into the cell. This is an alternative to using the Enter key or an Arrow key to enter the data into the spreadsheet. The third symbol, a function key, allows you to add a function to the cell entry by accessing the Function Wizard. The right part of the formula bar displays the contents of the selected cell. If the cell contains a formula, the formula bar displays the formula, and the cell itself in the worksheet displays the result of that formula.

The Worksheet Area

	A	B	C	D	E	F	G	H	I
1									
2									
3									
4									

The worksheet area of the spreadsheet is where data is entered. The worksheet is a grid or matrix of cells that is 256 columns wide by 16,384 rows long. Each of these many cells can contain text, numbers, formulas, or graphics. Each cell has its own name or address that consists of the column letter followed by the row number. The column letters (A, B, C,..., IV) are listed at the top of each column, and row numbers (1, 2, 3, ..., 16,384) are listed to the left of each row. Therefore, the cell in the upper left corner of the worksheet is referred to as cell A1, the cell immediately below A1 is referred to as cell A2, the cell to the right of A1 is cell B1, and so on. All spreadsheets use this same cell naming technique. The active cell (the one into which any input will be placed) can be identified by a solid black border around the cell which emphasizes that cell and makes it stand out from the others.

Sheet Tabs

Excel worksheets are stored in a format which combines multiple worksheets into one file known as a workbook. This new way of saving worksheets began with version 5.0 and has carried over to version 7.0. The new format allows several related worksheets to be contained in one file. Also, any charts that have been derived from a worksheet will be saved in that workbook or file. The sheet tabs, near the bottom of the screen, allow you to switch between worksheets and charts in a workbook. You may rename, copy, or delete any existing worksheet or chart or insert a new sheet or chart by clicking a sheet tab with your right mouse button and making a choice from the resulting menu.

Renaming a worksheet or chart can be very handy. Rather than calling a worksheet simply "Sheet 1" it may be better to call it something more descriptive such as "Budget" or "1stMonth." To rename a sheet double click on the sheet tab and type the new title.

The right- and left-pointing arrow buttons to the left of the sheet tabs are the sheet tab control buttons, which allow you to scroll through the list of sheet tabs either one at a time in either direction, or by going to the first sheet or the last sheet with just one click.

The Status Bar

Ready Sum=0

The status bar is located directly below the sheet tabs. It contains various pieces of information such as the current state of Excel, as well as some messages. For example, most of the time the message visible on the left end of the status bar is "Ready" indicating that Excel is waiting for input. But as soon as you begin to type data, the status bar lists "Enter" as your current message, replacing "Ready." As you scroll through the menus with the arrow keys, Excel will display a short message on the status bar describing the selected menu command. Also, as you will recall from earlier, if you point the mouse at a toolbar short-cut button, the status line will display a brief description of that button's function.

NAVIGATING THE WORKSHEET

Moving around an Excel spreadsheet can be accomplished in several ways, depending on the distance to be covered. If the active cell is located fairly close to your destination cell, use the arrow keys to move to the new cell. To use the arrow keys, simply press the appropriate key once for each cell that you wish to move across. For example, assuming that the current cell is A1 and you wish to move to cell A4, press the down arrow key three times. To move from A4 to E4 press the right arrow key four times.

> **Lotus Tip**
> In the Lotus program, pressing the "Home" key makes cell A1 the active cell. For example, if the active cell is H37 and you press the "Home" key one time, the cursor will move back to cell A1 in the spreadsheet.

On the other hand, moving to a more distant cell is usually easier with the mouse. When the mouse pointer is over the worksheet area, it will be in the shape of an outlined white cross. If the destination cell is visible on the screen, place the mouse pointer over that cell and click one time on the left mouse button to make it the new active cell. To move to a cell which is not currently displayed on the screen, click on the scroll bars until the cell is visible and then click on it.

For example, if the active cell is A1 and you wish to make A40 the active cell, merely click on the arrow at the bottom of the scroll bar on the right-hand part of the screen until A40 is visible. Move the mouse pointer over cell A40 and click with the left button. Each click on the scroll bar moves the worksheet up or down one page. The box in the scroll bar moves up and down to indicate your position in the worksheet. If you wish to move up, click above the box. If down, click beneath the box. To move more quickly, you can drag the box to the desired position, and Excel will let you know your location with a message on the left side of the formula bar.

If you know the name of the cell to which you wish to move (such as A40 in the example above) use the Goto command. The Goto command will change the active cell to whichever cell you indicate. To use this command, choose Edit Goto from the menu then type in the cell address to which you wish to move and press Enter. Cell A40 should now be visible on the screen and outlined. A short-cut method of accomplishing the same task is to press the function key **F5** and simply type in the destination cell address and press Enter.

Another way of moving around the worksheet is to use the Page Up (PgUp) and Page Down (PgDn) keys. These keys shift the viewable area up or down one screen at a time. The amount of change depends on the size of the computer screen. A notebook computer may only change by twenty rows each time PgUp or PgDn is pressed, but a full size monitor will display more rows and, therefore, shift up and down in larger increments. No matter what size screen you are working with, the pointer maintains its relative position on the screen. For example, if cell A1 is the active cell and you press PgDn, your row number will change, but the pointer will still be located in the A column.

ENTERING TEXT AND NUMBERS

To enter data into a cell, begin by choosing the cell you wish to use. Place the mouse pointer over the cell and press the left button once. This makes the cell the active or current cell, which means it will be the cell into which the data you type is entered. Type the data you wish to enter. Notice that as you type, the data appears in the cell itself and also on the formula bar. If you make a mistake while you are typing, use the backspace key or the delete key to remove the unwanted characters. When you are done typing, the data can be entered into the spreadsheet by pressing the Enter key.

Another way of entering the data is by pressing an arrow key instead of the Enter key. This can save time and keystrokes if you know into which cell your next entry will be placed. Suppose you are entering a long list of numbers into column A. After entering the first number in cell A1, rather than pressing the Enter key and then the down arrow key, simply press the down arrow key at the end of the entry and it will save you a keystroke. In this way, the number will be entered into cell A1 and the active cell will immediately shift to cell A2.

Data can be entered into a spreadsheet as labels, values, formulas, or functions. It is important to understand the different types of data, because labels can not be used in numerical calculations. A label can be one or more words or some combination of letters, symbols, or numbers. A label will be automatically aligned on the left side of the cell. Remember it is information that can not be included in calculations by the program. Examples of numbers that would be used as labels but would not be included in calculations are social security numbers, dates and phone numbers.

Values are numbers that are intended to have arithmetic operations performed on them. Values are automatically aligned starting at the right border of the cell and working back to the left, as if from an imaginary decimal point at the right cell boundary.

Correcting Errors

If you realize you have made an error in a cell after the data has been entered, there are ways to correct the entry. One way to correct the data is to return to the cell and simply retype the data. As you begin typing, the old entry is erased and the new information is entered into the cell.

If the entry in a cell is long, it would be tedious to retype the whole thing if you have only made a minor error. In this case, a better way to correct an entry is to use the Excel "Edit" key, which is the function key **F2**. To use this key, click on the cell you wish to correct to make it the active cell, then press **F2**. A flashing cursor will appear at the end of the entry in the cell itself, not in the formula bar. Use the arrow keys to move through the entry, then use the backspace or delete key to erase the error and type the correct characters. When you are finished, press Enter. *Pressing an arrow key to enter the data will not work when you are using the Edit mode of Excel.*

The Undo Command

Up to this point we have discussed how to correct a cell entry. Suppose, however, that you have accidentally deleted part of a spreadsheet, or some other action that is fairly major, but unintentional. What can you do? It would be tedious to type everything that you have deleted back into the spreadsheet, so instead use the Undo command available in Excel. Each time you choose Undo, the program backs up, to undo the last action requested.

> **Lotus Tip**
> In Lotus, the Undo command will only undo one step. Undo will not retrace multiple steps as it does in the Excel program.

Provided you have enough memory space, the program is capable of retracing up to 99 steps for you. This can be a life saver if you realize you have done something to your spreadsheet that you didn't mean to do. There are two ways to access the Undo command. Choose Edit Undo from the menus or click on the Undo icon located on the toolbar. The Undo icon is the button with a left-pointing arrow on it. Each time you choose this command from the menus or click on the icon on the toolbar, the program will undo one action.

Adjusting Column Width and Row Height

If the label or text you are entering into a cell is too wide for that cell, several things can happen. Suppose you wish to enter the text "My Monthly Budget" into a cell as a heading. That phrase is longer than the default column width in the spreadsheet, so the text will run over into the next cell. As long as the next cell is empty, Excel allows the text to run over and does not truncate it. But if there is a data entry of any kind in the next cell, the program will cut the new text from view. The full text is still entered into the cell, and it will appear in its entirety in the formula bar, but it will not be visible totally in the cell, since it will be truncated because of the next entry.

> **Lotus Tip**
> The Lotus program also notifies you that the number does not fit in the column, but rather than pound signs, it displays a series of asterisks at the top of the cell. The number will only appear in the cell if you adjust the column width to accommodate it.

It is usually obvious when text is truncated, but truncating numbers could lead to confusion. To avoid this problem, when the column is too narrow to display a number Excel converts the number to a series of pound signs (######). This is your cue to adjust the column width.

> **Lotus Tip**
>
> In Lotus, the equivalent menu command for Excel's "Format" is "Style." For example, to adjust the column width in Lotus, choose Style Column Width from the menus.

If you want the text or value to be contained totally in one cell, the column width can be adjusted to allow this. There are several ways to adjust the column width in Excel. One way to accomplish this is to click on the column letter heading to highlight the entire column. Then choose Format (note that you must use the "o" rather than the "F" in this case if you are using the "Alt" key rather than the mouse, since "F" is used for the "File" menu option) Column Width from the menus and type in the exact number of spaces you wish the column width to be. To use this method, simply make an educated guess as to how wide the column should be to accommodate the entry.

An easier way to adjust the column width is to place the mouse pointer over the right boundary of the column heading you wish to adjust. The pointer will become a black cross when you are directly over the column boundary. Hold the left mouse button down and drag the column boundary to the width you wish it to be, either narrower or wider. Release the mouse button when the width is correct. For example, if you want to widen column C in this manner, place the mouse pointer over the boundary between the column C and column D headings until you have a black cross showing. Then hold down the left mouse button and drag the column boundary to the right until you have the width you desire. To narrow the column simply drag the mouse pointer to the left. Notice that as you are dragging the mouse, the reference area of the formula bar displays the exact width of the column as you change it.

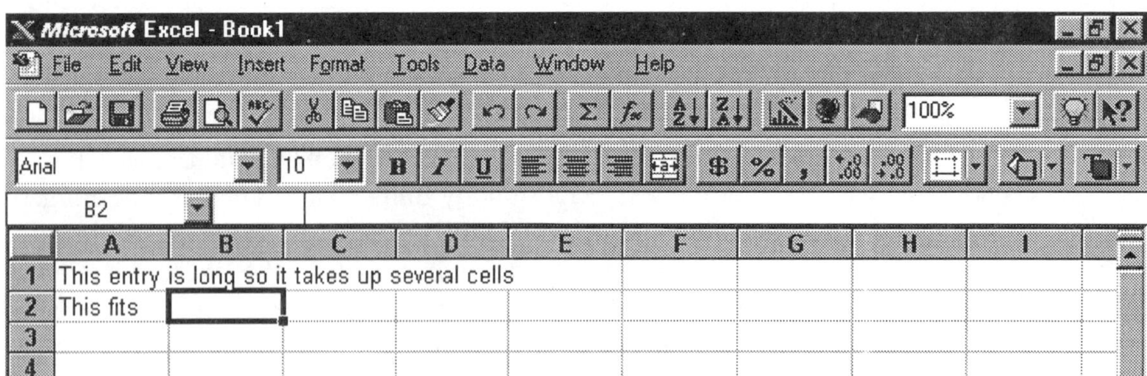

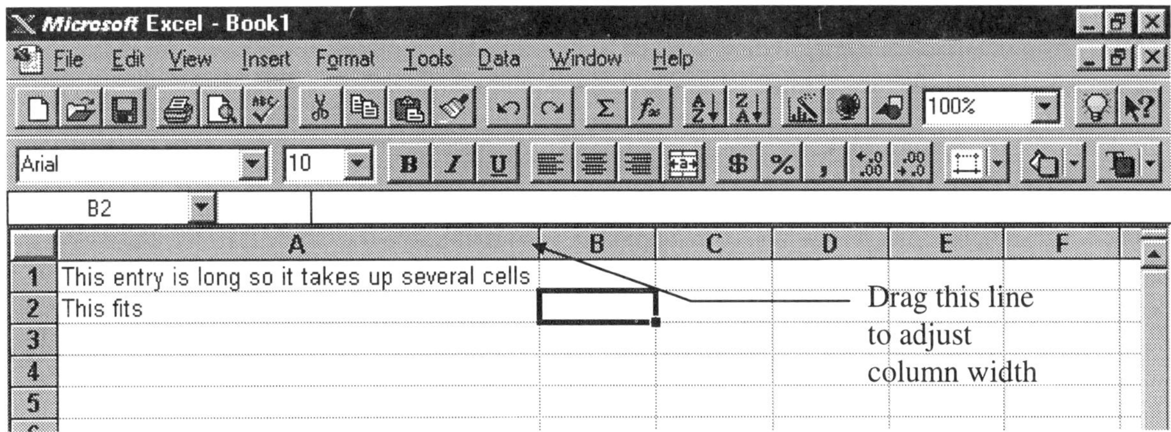

Excel also allows you to adjust a column's width according to the longest entry in that column. Suppose you wish to do this to column A. Type your entries into the column, then place the mouse pointer over the boundary between the column A and the column B headings until you have a black cross. Then double click the left mouse button. The program will adjust the column width to the length of the longest entry in that column. If longer entries are added in this column after this adjustment has been made, it must be redone.

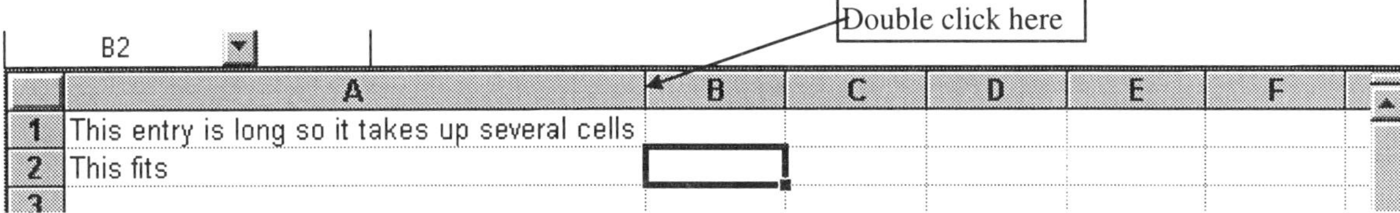

The row height can be adjusted in a spreadsheet in the same ways the column width can be adjusted. Follow the same steps involved in column width adjustment, but instead of using the column letter headings, use the row number headings at the left to make the adjustments.

Formatting Cells

You can change the look of your spreadsheet by changing the format of the cells. Excel lets you adjust the size the look of text, the alignment of text and numbers and even the color of the spreadsheet.

Fonts

Once you have entered labels or values into a spreadsheet, any number of changes can be made in the appearance of those entries if you don't like the way they look. Excel has many formatting and alignment options available. Formatting refers to the appearance of the data. A "typeface" is a particular style of drawing letters and numbers. Excel has many styles available for use in its spreadsheets such as Times New Roman, Arial, and Courier. The typeface you choose is simply a matter of personal taste. Typeface also refers to whether the text is drawn **bold**, *italics*, or perhaps ***bold italics***.

The term "type size" refers to the size of the typeface. When typewriters were commonly used, type size was defined in characters per inch (CPI). This convention was somewhat confusing because the larger the CPI number, the smaller was the text. Today, with computers we normally refer to the type size in "points." Each point represents an increment of 1/72nd of an inch, so there are 72 points to the inch. A typeface printed at a 12 point size is larger than the same typeface printed at a size of 10 points.

Generally, we refer to the typeface and type size combination as a font. So when we say "change the font to 12 point bold Times New Roman," it is understood that we are referring to a particular typeface (Times New Roman, bolded) and type size (12 point).

Alignment

The alignment of the data means the data's position within the cell and is also part of the format. Remember that Excel, by default, displays text at the left side of a cell and numbers at the right side of a cell. Sometimes this is not the most attractive way to display the data in a worksheet. We can easily change the way that these entries are displayed through the use of alignment options. Excel provides three different horizontal alignments within a cell. We can have the text or numbers aligned with the left or right sides of the cell or centered within the cell boundaries.

Excel also allows centering of text across more than one column of cells. To accomplish this, type the text into the leftmost cell that will be used. Then highlight from that cell to the right to include all the columns across which you wish the text to be centered. Click on the icon that looks like an "a" with arrows on each side. The text will then be centered across the columns you have chosen. If, instead, you choose the regular centering icon, the text will simply be centered within one cell.

> **Lotus Tip**
>
> To center text across columns in Lotus, type the text into the leftmost cell, highlight the range you want the text to occupy, then choose Style Alignment Center Across columns. In this way, Lotus will allow you to center across columns, just as Excel does.

Formatting numbers

Just as labels can be changed, the appearance of the numbers in your spreadsheet can be changed also. Numbers can be displayed in any typeface and point size you wish to use. To change the appearance of a number, click on that cell to make it the active cell, then click on whatever typeface and point size you want from the toolbar.

In addition to font changes, the appearance of numbers can also be altered by adding commas and dollar signs and by changing the number of decimal places displayed. To make these changes, begin by making the cell you want to change the active cell. From the menus choose Format Cells and then Numbers from the selections available. Choose the category desired from the box on the left side of the dialog box. Depending on what category you choose, other options will be available. If you choose "Number," you can set the number of decimal places displayed and whether commas will appear or not. You can also choose how negative numbers will appear in your spreadsheet. Negative numbers can be displayed in a different color type, using the negative sign, or using parentheses. If you select the category "Currency," you can also choose whether to have dollar signs or not.

Using Ranges

When working with spreadsheets, you may want to perform an operation on an area of the sheet that encompasses more than just one cell. Any rectangular grouping of cells is called a range. Think of a range as being just an area of the spreadsheet. A range can be one row extending across many columns, one column running down several rows, or a block that covers many rows and many columns. A range is defined by listing the two cells that are diagonally opposite from each other and placing a colon (:) between them, such as the range A1:H8.

> **Lotus Tip**
> In Lotus, a range is defined by listing the two cells that are diagonally opposite from each other and placing two periods between them, such as the range A1..H8.

Selecting a Range

Suppose you wish to make a particular change to a large number of cells in your spreadsheet. It would be tedious to change one cell at a time, especially over a large area of the sheet. Instead it would be more practical to simultaneously select the whole range and perform the changes all at once. To select or highlight a contiguous range, place the mouse pointer over a corner cell in the range, press the left button and drag the mouse in whichever direction will encompass the entire range you need, then release the mouse button. As you drag the mouse, notice the reference area of the formula bar. Excel shows you the dimensions of the range being selected.

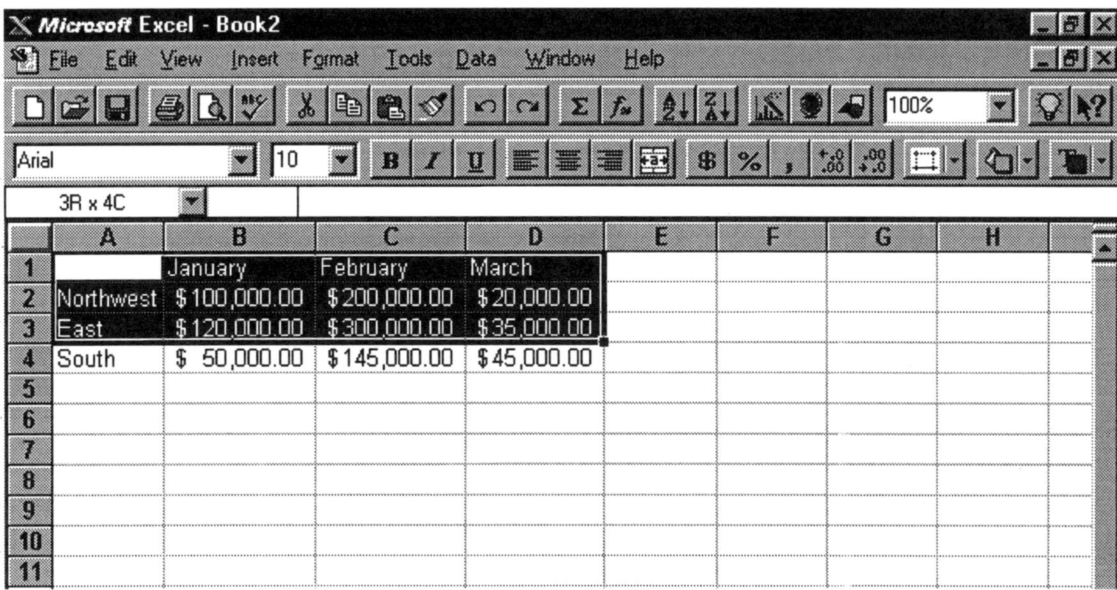

You can also use the keyboard to select a range. First change the active cell to a corner cell of the range to be selected, press and hold down the Shift key, and use the arrow keys to move in whatever directions will highlight the entire range. Note that if you release the Shift key while pressing an arrow key you will lose the highlighting.

Selecting Non-contiguous Ranges

At times you may also need to select a non-contiguous range (two or more unconnected ranges) of cells. To do this, simply select the first range as you normally would, and then hold down the Control key as you select the other ranges that you need.

C1 | February

	A	B	C	D
1		January	February	March
2	Northwest	$ 100,000.00	$ 200,000.00	$ 20,000.00
3	East	$ 120,000.00	$ 300,000.00	$ 35,000.00
4	South	$ 50,000.00	$ 145,000.00	$ 45,000.00
5				

Hold the control key down while selecting this column

It is very important that you be allowed to select cells in Excel since, like most other Windows applications, Excel works in the "select, then act" mode. In Excel, you first select the cells that you wish to act on, then choose the operation that you want to perform. This would seem to be a minor point, but it is actually quite important. In the "select, then act" method, the cells stay selected after the operation has been performed, thereby allowing another operation on those cells without re-selecting them. For example, if you decide to change the font and the alignment of a range of cells, you need only highlight that range once. As long as the range remains highlighted, you can continue performing operations on those cells until you are satisfied with their appearance. To turn off the highlighting, simply click the mouse anywhere outside the highlighted range.

SAVING YOUR SPREADSHEET

One of the most important things to remember about working with personal computers is to save your work . . . **OFTEN**. When you load a spreadsheet program and begin using it, the worksheet on your screen is located in RAM, the part of your computer's memory that depends on a constant flow of electricity to continue. If the power is accidentally shut off to your machine, anything that you were working on that was not saved onto disk is lost. So to avoid the frustration of losing your work, save frequently. Saving a document takes only a moment and can prevent hours of redoing work that you have lost.

Saving Your Spreadsheet For The First Time And Subsequent Times

The first time you save a spreadsheet, you must tell the computer where you want the work saved and what you want to call it. To save, choose File Save from the menus and then, by clicking with the mouse, choose the physical location where you want the document to be saved, such as in the C drive (hard drive) of your machine or on a 3 ½ inch floppy disk. Then type the name you want to use for the spreadsheet into the box for File Name and click on the Save button in the dialog box. At this point, a message will appear in the status bar of your screen saying that the program is saving your spreadsheet under the name you have chosen to call it. When the computer is finished saving the document, this message disappears and you are ready to continue to work on the spreadsheet.

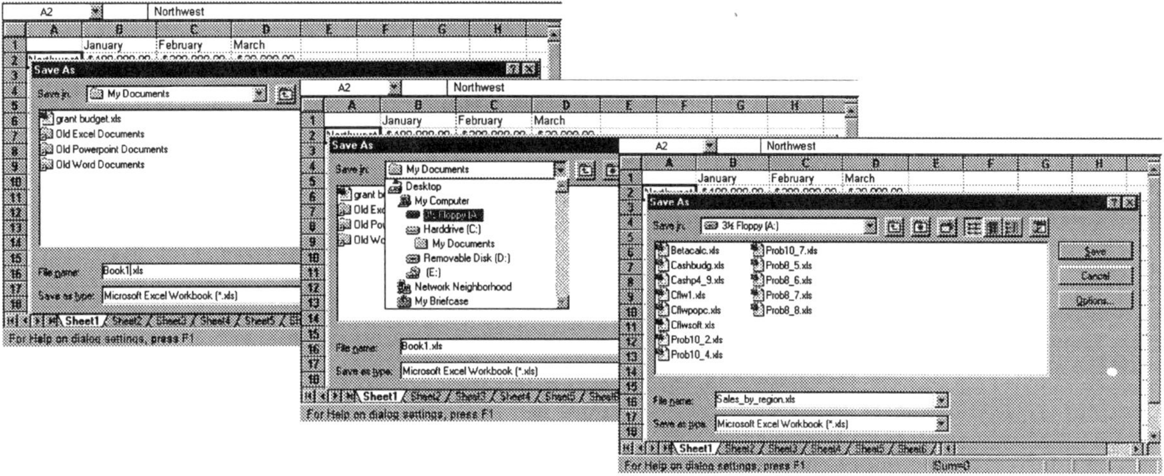

When additions or changes have been made to the spreadsheet, it should be saved again so that these changes will not be lost if there is a power failure. Once you have done the initial save, subsequent saves are easy. Simply choose File Save from the menus again, but this time the computer will skip directly to the save process and bypass asking you where to put the document and what to call it. The program assumes you want the work saved in the same location and under the same name as before. This is called a "Quick Save" and it takes only a matter of seconds to save the work you have done since the last save process was executed. This is time well spent.

You can also execute the Save command by clicking with the mouse on the Save button on the toolbar. Remember, the icons on the toolbar represent short-cut methods of executing commands. The Save icon is a picture of a floppy disk. If you have not saved the worksheet yet, clicking on this icon will lead you to the dialog box that allows you to choose the location and name for the document. If you have done the initial save already, clicking on the icon executes a Quick Save. The same results can be accomplished by either using the menus or the icon.

> **Lotus Tip**
> The Save icon in Lotus is a picture of an open file folder with an arrow pointing downward into the folder.

Saving In Another Location Or Under A Different Name

Another feature offered by Excel with regard to saving your spreadsheet is the "Save As" option. Suppose you have saved a worksheet, then decide that you also wish to save it in another physical location in your computer or you want to save it again but under a different name. If you click on File Save again, the computer will execute a quick save, simply saving the document again in the same location and under the same name. Instead, click on File Save As from the menus. The dialog box will appear that again allows you to choose where you want the document saved and what you want to call it. You can change the location, the name, or both. From this point forward, however, if you execute a quick save, the document will be saved in this new location or under the new name, whatever you have changed. If you also want it saved again in the old location or under the old name, you must execute another File Save As and save it there too.

USING EXCEL FORMULAS

The real benefit of a spreadsheet program is its ability to use formulas to calculate data. A formula expresses relationships among values in a worksheet. Formulas are based on cell addresses in the spreadsheet. For example, to add two cells together, we simply tell the program to take the contents of one cell and add that to the contents of the second cell. The formula for accomplishing this task is entered into the cell in which we want the answer to appear.

Entering Excel Formulas

In Excel, all formulas begin with the equals sign (=) to indicate to the program that a formula will follow. Without the equals sign, the program will treat the formula as text and will not calculate a result. The operators +, -, *, /, and ^ mean add, subtract, multiply, divide, and exponent respectively when used in a formula. For example, typing the formula =A1+A2 into cell A3 tells the program to add the contents of cell A1 to the contents of cell A2 and display the sum in cell A3. Remember, the cell A3 will contain the answer, but the formula bar will contain the formula. The contents of cells A1 and A2 must be either values, formulas, or functions. The cells may also be blank, which would be treated like zeros.

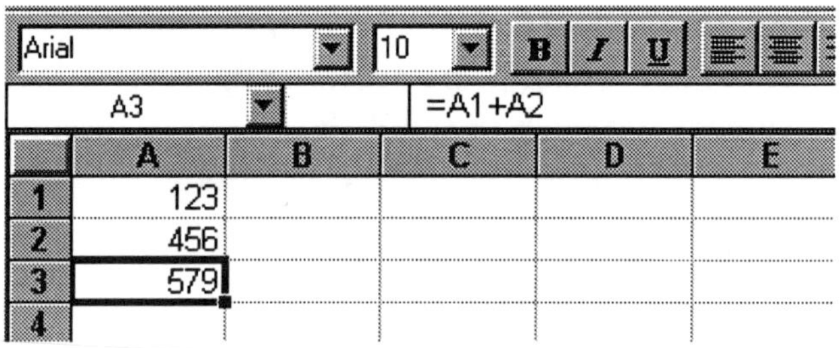

Arial | 10 | B | I | U

A3 | =A1+A2

	A	B	C	D	E
1	123				
2	456				
3	579				
4					

Another way to enter a formula into a cell is to use the pointer method. This involves using the mouse to point to cells that we want in the formula. To add the contents of cells A1 and A2 using the pointer method, start by clicking on cell A3, where the formula is to be inserted. Then type the equals sign, point at A1 and click, type the plus sign, point at A2 and click, then hit Enter. Notice as you did this, the formula bar displayed each cell and sign as you worked. This method will give you the same result as typing the formula directly into the cell. It is an easier method to use if one or more of the cells you want included in your formula are outside the viewable area of your spreadsheet. In this case, to enter the formula directly into the cell, you would have to know the cell addresses you are including. With the pointer method, you can start your formula at a cell you know, then move the mouse to the other cells that may be off your screen.

Using Parentheses To Control Order Of Operations

Using the mathematical operators +, -, *, /, and ^ seems fairly straightforward, but in some cases it is more complicated than it appears. For example, let's say we want Excel to evaluate the following equation:

$$X = 3 + 4 / 2$$

If Excel simply worked through the equation from left to right, the answer would be 3.5. But Excel does not work that way. Excel evaluates equations using a procedure called operator precedence, which means that certain mathematical operators take precedence over others. Normally, exponents are calculated first. Multiplication and division are usually performed next, but they are equal in precedence so these operations will be performed from left to right in the equation. Finally addition and subtraction, which are also equal in precedence, are performed.

Keeping in mind that Excel works in this manner, look at the equation again. The division would be performed first, then the addition. So the answer, according to Excel, would be 5, very different from the answer we would assume if the program simply worked from left to right in the equation. But suppose for our purposes the equation will only be correct if the addition is performed first, then the division. To force Excel to perform the operations in the order we prefer, we can add parentheses to our equation, thus modifying the order of precedence. Operations that are enclosed in parentheses are always evaluated first. Modified, our equation would look like this:

$$X = (3 + 4) / 2$$

The parentheses force Excel to perform the addition first, then the division. In this way, we can be sure that we achieve the results that are valid in our situation. If you are in doubt use parentheses.

Using Built-in Excel Functions In Formulas

The Excel program has functions built into it that can be used in formulas. Functions are certain words such as SUM and AVERAGE that can be typed into formulas, telling the program to perform those tasks, without having to describe how to do those tasks to the computer. For example, by typing in the word AVERAGE, the program understands that it should add the contents of all the cells involved, then divide that total by the number of entries. The user does not have to explain to the computer what an average is since it is a built-in function of the program. These functions make it easier to build complex equations. Functions also cut down on the amount of information that must be keyed in, reducing the likelihood of errors. To use a function, choose the term that describes what task is to be performed and supply the proper cell addresses to be included. For example, to add cells A1, A2, A3, A4, and A5 and put the total in cell A6 we could just use plus signs, but that would be a fairly tedious equation to type into the cell, and an error-prone way of accomplishing this task.

= A1 + A2 + A3 + A4 + A5

Instead, by using a built-in Excel function, we can simplify the equation and minimize the amount of information that must be keyed into the cell. The same equation, using a function, would look like this:

= SUM (A1 : A5)

Lotus Tip
Lotus also has built in functions, but they are called @Functions, since the "@" symbol must precede the function word. Remember also that in Lotus, two periods separate the cells defining a range. For example, to add the contents of cells A1 through A8, the formula in Lotus would be

=@SUM(A1..A8)

The equation must still begin with the equals sign, to tell Excel it will be calculating something, then the function SUM, then within parentheses the range of cells to be included. The true value of this method of writing a formula becomes apparent when large strings of cells must be included. It is much more efficient and less error-prone to simply type in the first and last cell in the string, rather than having to include each individual cell address in the equation.

You can also accomplish this same task by typing part of the formula and pointing with the mouse at the cell addresses to be included. To do this, click on the cell where the formula with the function is to be inserted, then type the equals sign and the word SUM followed by an opening parenthesis. Then click on the first cell in the range, type a colon, click on the last cell to complete the range and press the Enter key.

Using the Excel Function Wizard

Using functions in Excel can be very confusing. Many of the financial functions have several parameters that must be specified. To make it easier to use functions in formulas, Excel provides the Function Wizard, which is a step by step series of dialog boxes that lead you through the process of choosing the function you need and entering the necessary information. A function can be simply typed into a cell without the Function Wizard, but it is there for you if you need the assistance.

To use the Function Wizard, click on the cell into which you wish to enter the function and then type the equals sign. Click on the function button (f_x) in the formula bar. At this point, step one of the Function Wizard will appear as a dialog box on your screen. Choose the category of function you wish to enter, such as financial, statistical, etc. An alphabetical list of the functions available under that category will appear. As you scroll through the functions available, a short description of each of the functions will appear in the dialog box. Choose the function you need, then click on the "Next" button at the bottom of the dialog box. The second Function Wizard dialog box will appear allowing you

Lotus Tip
Using functions can also be confusing in Lotus, but the program does provide helpful ways to deal with functions. By typing the equals sign, then the "@" symbol and then pressing the F3 function key, a dialog box will appear that lists the functions available in Lotus. Choose the one you want and it will appear in your cell along with the parameters required to fulfill the function. Another option when using functions is to type the equals sign into your cell, then click on the "@" symbol on the formula bar. At this point a dialog box will appear that allows you to choose from a few common functions or choose "List All." Choose the function you want and it will appear in your cell.

to insert the information needed for your function. When you are done specifying the parameters needed, click on the "Finish" button at the bottom of the dialog box.

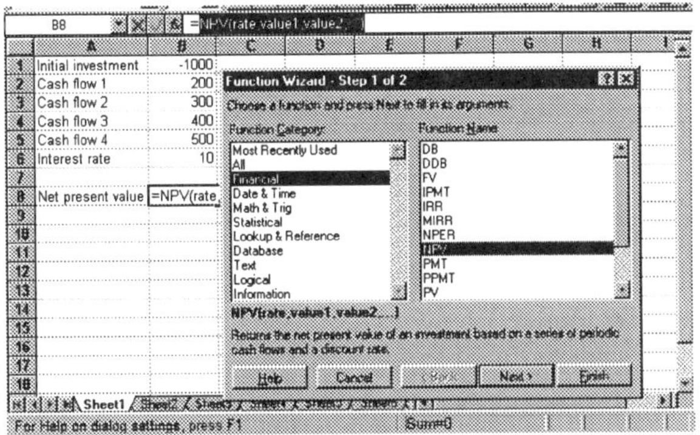

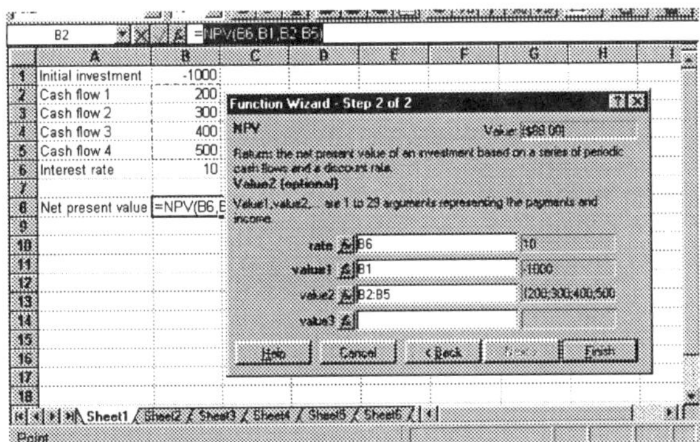

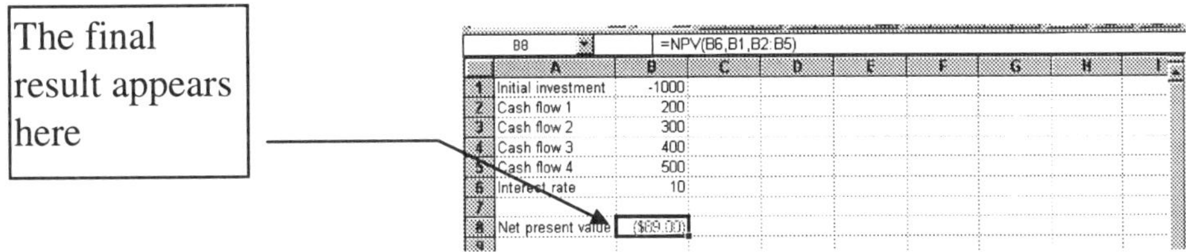

Examples of Functions

Excel has hundreds of functions built into the program, many of which are financial functions. The following is a list of the *financial* functions available in Excel 7.0. They are listed in alphabetical order in the Function Wizard under the category "Financial."

DB	Returns the depreciation of an asset for a specified period using the fixed-declining balance method.
DDB	Returns the depreciation of an asset for a specified period using the double-declining balance method or some other method you specify.
FV	Returns the future value of an investment.

IPMT	Returns the interest payment for an investment for a given period.
IRR	Returns the internal rate of return for a series of cash flows.
MIRR	Returns the internal rate of return where positive and negative cash flows are financed at different rates.
NPER	Returns the number of periods for an investment.
NPV	Returns the net present value of an investment based on a series of periodic cash flows and a discount rate.
PMT	Returns the periodic payment for an annuity.
PPMT	Returns the payment on the principal for an investment for a given period.
PV	Returns the present value of an investment.
RATE	Returns the interest rate per period of an annuity.
SLN	Returns the straight-line depreciation of an asset for one period.
SYD	Returns the sum-of-years' digits depreciation of an asset for a specified period.
VDB	Returns the depreciation of an asset for a specified or partial period using a declining balance method.

Copying and Moving Formulas

Some users feel that the copy functions are what make electronic spreadsheets so valuable. Some formulas in Excel can be rather long and detailed. The last thing you want to do is retype a formula over and over again if the same formula is necessary in several rows or columns of your spreadsheet. Luckily, Excel allows us to copy a formula from one cell to another. Copying leaves the cell contents in the original cell, but also places it in the new cell. It is equally frustrating to enter a formula into a cell and realize that it is in the wrong location. Excel also allows the contents of cells to be moved. Moving the contents of a cell involves eliminating what is in the original cell and placing the contents only in the new location.

Relative versus Absolute Cell Addressing

As a formula is copied, Excel automatically updates the cell addresses used in the formula to maintain the same relative relationships. For example, if you need to add cells A1 through A15 and want the answer in cell A16, you would type the formula =SUM(A1:A15) into cell A16. But suppose you also want to add cells B1 through B15 and put that sum in cell B16. Rather than retyping the formula into cell B16, simply copy the formula from A16 to B16. When you copy the formula, however, it will appear in cell B16 as =SUM(B1:B15).

This is called *relative cell addressing*. When the program copies the formula, it holds the same relative relationship intact. The formula requested that the contents of the fifteen cells directly above it be summed. When the formula was copied to the column next door, the intent of the formula remained the same. So the program adjusts the cell addresses and sums the fifteen cells directly above the formula, in this case in column B rather than A.

There are times when you copy a formula from one cell to another, but you don't want the cell references to change, instead you want them held constant. Excel allows cell references to be held constant by inserting dollar signs in the appropriate places in the formula. Holding the cell references constant is called *absolute cell addressing*. Suppose each time you use a formula, you need the computer to look up certain information from a table you have constructed in your spreadsheet. As you copy that formula from one row down to the next row, you don't want that cell reference to adjust down, you want it held constant so that it will continue to look up the information it needs in the table. In this case, a formula might look like this:

= HLOOKUP ($D$4 : $E$8)

The dollar signs inserted in front of the column letters and row numbers tell the program that as that formula is copied to other locations in the spreadsheet, it is not to allow the cell references to adjust. The same data is needed in each cell that uses this formula. In this example, both the columns and the rows have been held constant. It is also possible to hold just the columns constant, or just the rows, depending on what is needed in your spreadsheet.

Copying Cells and Ranges of Cells

No matter what a cell contains, the contents can be copied to other cells if necessary. For our purposes, we will look at copying formulas, but keep in mind that any type of entry in a cell can be copied to other cells, not just formulas. There are several ways to copy a formula from one cell to another. One way involves clicking on the formula cell to make it active, then choosing **E**dit **C**opy from the menus. Click on the cell you wish to copy the formula into and choose **E**dit **P**aste from the menus. The formula will be copied to the new cell, leaving it intact in the original cell.

Another way to copy a formula involves dragging with the mouse. Suppose you have typed a formula into a cell and you need the same formula copied to the ten contiguous rows beneath it. The easy way to copy this formula is to click on the formula cell to make it active, then place your mouse over the bottom right corner of the cell where a small black box is visible. If your mouse is in the correct position, a black cross will replace the normal white cross. Click and hold the left mouse button and drag the mouse across the cells you want to contain the copied formula, releasing the mouse button when you are finished. The formula will be copied to all the cells over which the mouse was dragged.

> **Lotus Tip**
> To copy the contents of a cell in Lotus, place the mouse at the bottom right corner of the cell to be copied. A white arrow will appear and to the right and below it black points will also appear. Click and hold the left mouse button and drag the mouse across the cells you want to copy the formula into, releasing the mouse button when you are finished.

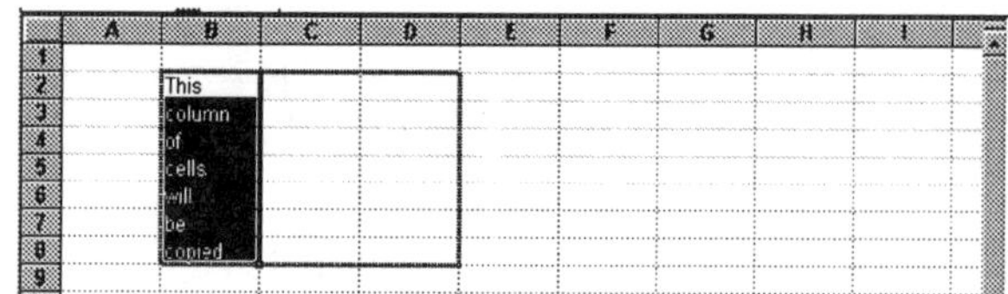

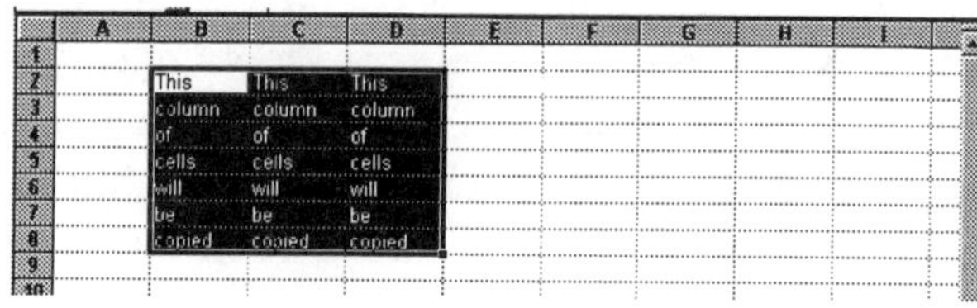

In addition to just copying one cell, Excel allows ranges of cells to be copied. To copy a whole range or area of a spreadsheet, click and drag the mouse across the range to be copied so that it becomes highlighted. Choose Edit Copy from the menus. Click on the upper left cell representing the new range and then choose Edit Paste from the menus. The information will remain in the original location and will also be copied to the new location.

Moving Cells and Ranges of Cells

Formulas can also be moved as well as copied. To move a formula, click on the formula's cell to make it active, then choose Edit Cut from the menus, click on the cell you wish to contain the formula, and choose Edit Paste from the menus. The formula will now appear only in the new cell, since it has been cut or moved from the original cell.

Whole ranges or areas of information can be moved as well as just individual cells. Click and drag with the mouse to highlight the range to be moved. Choose Edit Cut from the menus, click on the upper left corner cell of the area you wish the information moved into, and choose Edit Paste from the menus. The information will no longer exist in the old range, but will appear in the new range intact.

An alternative method to move cells is by highlighting the range to move and positioning the pointer midway beside and to the *right* of the range. With pointer so positioned, click and hold the left mouse button and drag the range to a new location. A shadow box will follow the mouse movement to show where you are moving the range.

> Lotus Tip
> To move the contents of a cell in Lotus, with the cell active, point at the upper cell boundary until the mouse pointer becomes a hand. Then click and drag the cell to the new location and release. The cell contents will be cut out of the original location and deposited in the new location.

CREATING EXCEL CHARTS

Spreadsheets are wonderful tools for organizing data, but they can be difficult to understand quickly by those who have not helped build them. Creating a graphic from the data in a spreadsheet can capture peoples' interest much more quickly than presenting the same information in spreadsheet form. A graphic can also better illustrate trends in the data that otherwise might be difficult to see if the spreadsheet has a large number of entries to muddle through. A graphic display of data can often be a much more pleasant way to view information.

Until recently, separate programs were needed to create graphics, since spreadsheet programs had no built-in graphic capabilities of their own. Excel is an integrated program, meaning the graphic capability we need is included in the spreadsheet program and no other program is necessary to build a chart.

> **Lotus Tip**
> Lotus is also an integrated program. Refer to the appendix for instructions on how to create charts in the Lotus program.

Using the Excel Chart Wizard

The Excel Chart Wizard is a series of dialog boxes that guide you step by step through the transformation of spreadsheet data into a graphic or chart. Each dialog box will ask for certain information to be provided so that the program can create the chart. Once the steps in the Chart Wizard are complete, the newly created chart can be formatted so that it looks exactly the way you want it to look.

Selecting The Data And Location Of The Chart

The first step in creating a chart in Excel is to select the desired data from the spreadsheet. To select the data, click and drag with the mouse to highlight the rows or columns you wish to chart. Remember if you wish to include non-contiguous ranges of the spreadsheet in your chart, highlight the first section as you normally would, then to highlight other sections press the Control key on the keyboard and highlight the information. If you do not hold down the control key while highlighting the additional data, the original data's highlighting will turn off and your information will not be selected.

Once the data has been selected, choose **I**nsert C**h**art from the menus. Another menu will appear that gives two options for creating the chart. By choosing "On this sheet" the chart will be created, saved and displayed directly on top of the spreadsheet from which the data is taken. This is called an embedded chart because the chart is embedded within the worksheet.

Once you have clicked on this option, the mouse becomes a black cross with a small chart icon attached to it. Move the mouse until it is located where you want the upper left corner of the chart to appear on the spreadsheet and click once. Your chart will now be created in this location.

By choosing the option labeled "As new sheet," the chart can be created as a separate window. By clicking on this option, the program takes you directly to the Chart Wizard.

You do not choose where to put the chart since this option will automatically create the chart as a whole new window.

Selecting The Chart Style And Titles

Once you have selected the data and chosen the location for your chart, the first dialog box from the Chart Wizard will appear on your screen. Step One in the Chart Wizard asks you if the selected data is correct. If you are satisfied that you have highlighted the correct data from your spreadsheet, click on the button labeled "Next" located at the bottom of the dialog box.

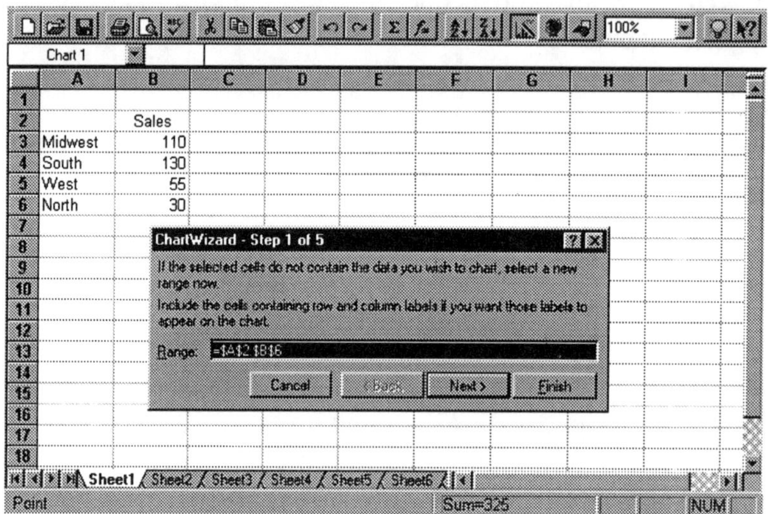

Step Two offers a choice of several different chart styles such as column, line, pie, 3-D, etc. The default chart style in Excel is the column chart. In other words, if you do not specify a chart style, the program will automatically create your chart as a column chart. Choose the style you wish to use, then click "Next" at the bottom of the dialog box.

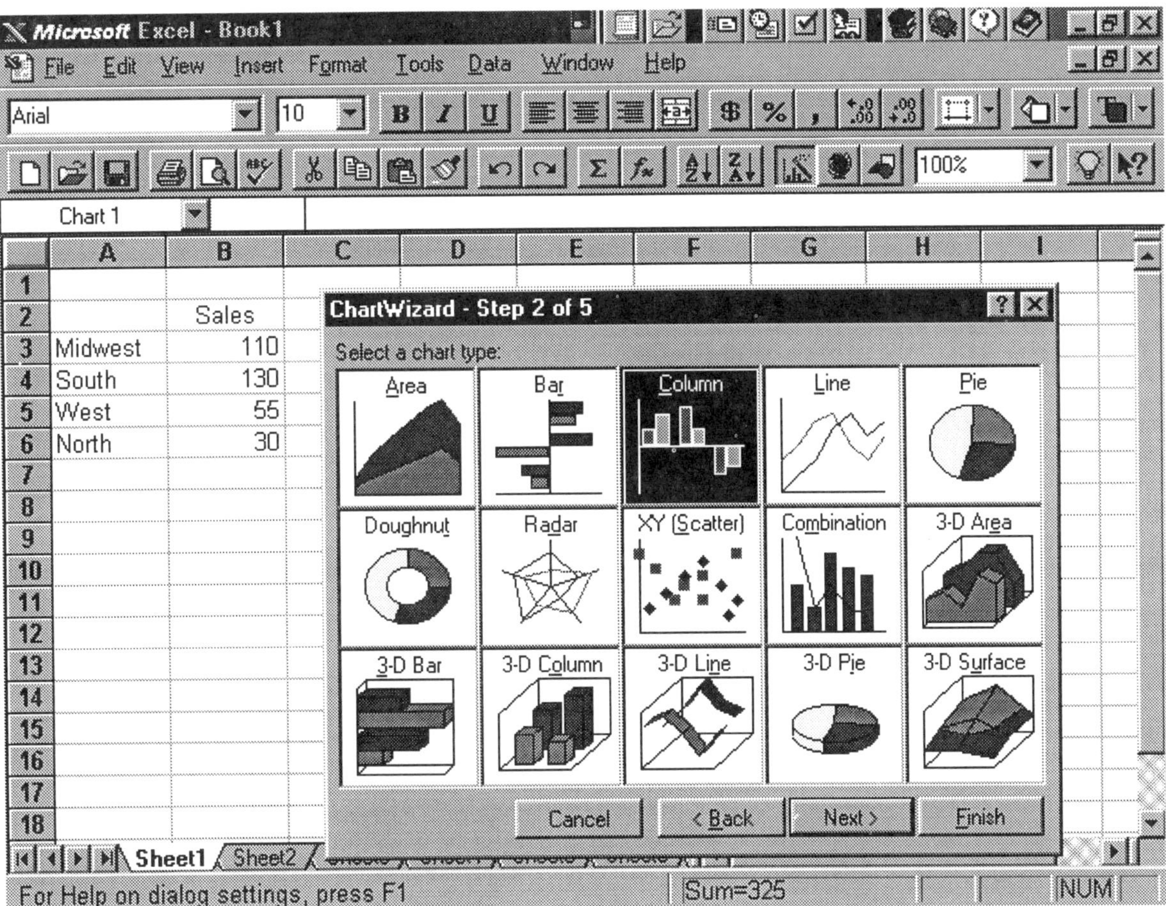

The third dialog box allows you to further define exactly what style of chart you want. For example, if you choose column as your style in Step 2, in Step 3 you will be given a choice of ten different column chart styles, some with chains connecting the columns, some with gridlines, etc. Choose the style you wish and continue by clicking "Next" again. Step 4 gives you a sample chart that shows how your chart will basically look and asks about the axis labeling. Usually Excel has defined this labeling for you correctly, so accept their default settings and move on by clicking on the "Next" button.

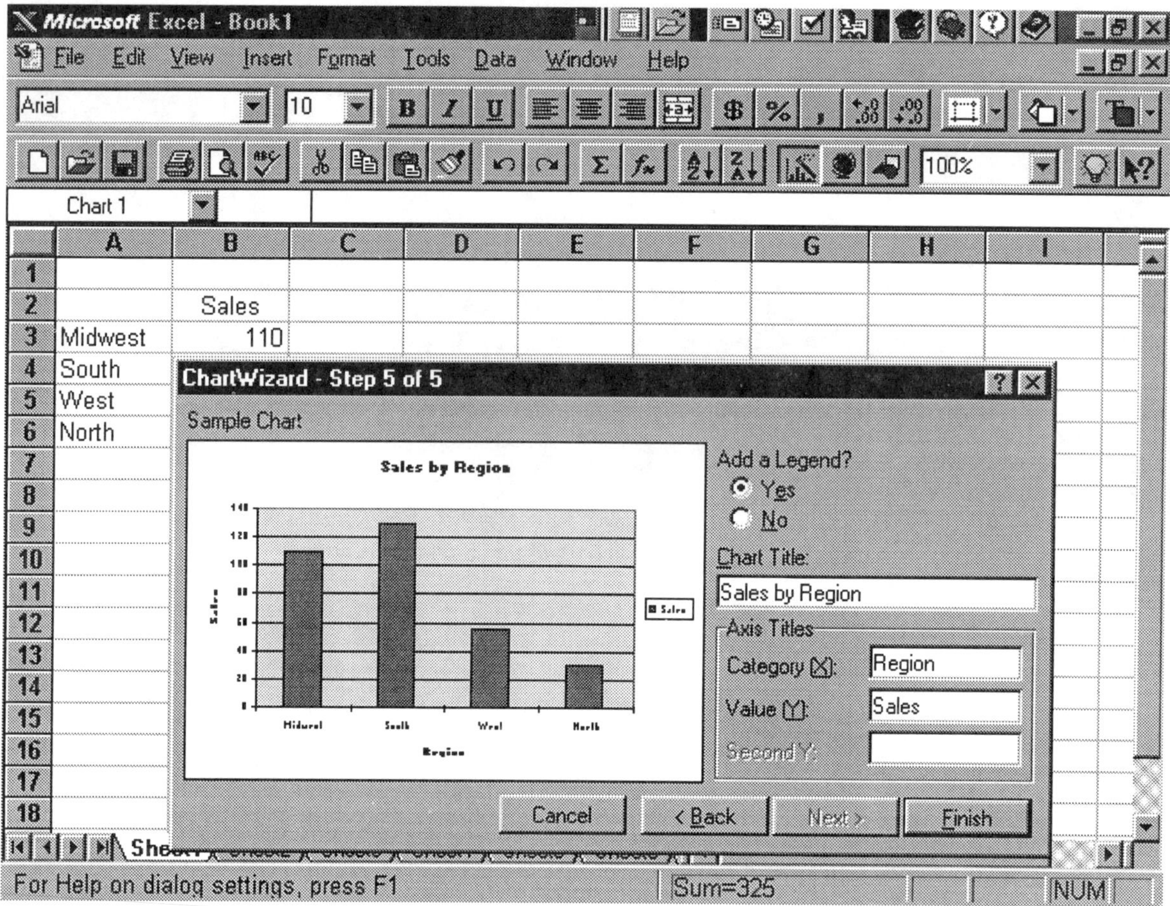

Finally, the last dialog box or Step 5 of the Chart Wizard appears on your screen with the sample chart visible. This step covers several items that will make the chart more understandable. First, a legend can be included or omitted, depending on personal preference. Also, the chart and the axes can be given titles. To add a title to the chart, move the mouse so that it is pointing at the title box, click the left button one time to place a flashing cursor in the box, and type the title you want for the chart. After typing in the title, DO NOT PRESS THE ENTER KEY. If you do, the Chart Wizard will close and you will not be able to enter axis titles at this time.

Instead of pressing Enter, once you have typed the title, press the Tab key one time to move your cursor to the X axis title box. Type the label that is appropriate for that axis. Remember the X axis is the horizontal or category axis on your chart. After typing this title, press the Tab key once again to move the cursor to the Y axis label box. The Y axis is the vertical or value axis on the chart. Type an appropriate entry for this axis. Then click the "Finish" button at the bottom of the dialog box. You have now completed the Chart Wizard. If your chart was created embedded in the spreadsheet, it will appear with the spreadsheet data in the background. If instead you chose to create the chart as a separate sheet, the spreadsheet will disappear from view and only the chart will be visible in its own new window on your screen.

If you did not add all the titles you needed to your chart while you were in the Chart Wizard (maybe you pressed ENTER after typing your chart title), all is not lost. Choose Insert Titles from the menus and then click on the appropriate boxes for the titles you want to add. Click on "OK" and you are returned to your chart. The program has now added a text area wherever you requested one in the previous step. Simply click once on the title box and type in the title you want to add. Follow the same procedure to type the axes titles if they are being added at this point also.

Suppose you have just constructed a column chart using the Chart Wizard and you realize that the chart would look better as another style of chart. With your mouse pointing anywhere in the chart, click the right button one time. A menu box will appear that allows you to select the chart type again. Select the style you want, click on "OK" and your chart will reappear on your screen as the new style rather than as a column chart.

Formatting The Chart

Once the Chart Wizard is complete, many things can be done to a chart to change its appearance. This is called formatting the chart. In Excel, each different item or element in the chart, such as the titles, the axes, or the labels, is treated as a separate "object" and can be selected and edited independently from the other items.

There are two different ways to select an item for editing. One way to edit requires that you simply point at the item with the mouse and double click the left mouse button. The Excel program is very sophisticated. It understands what item you have double clicked and knows what can be done to that item in terms of editing it. The program responds to the double click by bringing up a dialog box which presents the appropriate menus for formatting the item you have selected.

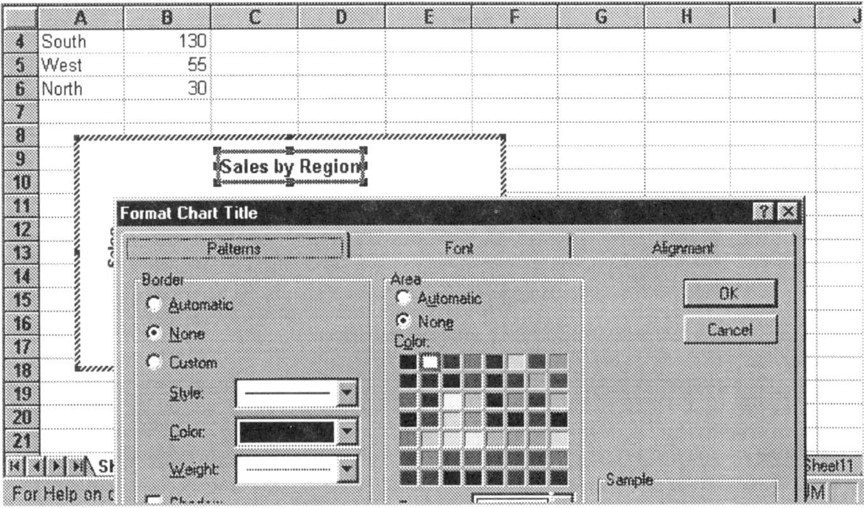

For example, if you want to change the font of the chart title, simply point the mouse at the title, double click the left button, and a dialog box will appear on the screen that is titled "Format Chart Title." This dialog box presents menus allowing you to select "Patterns,"

"Font," or "Alignment." By selecting "Font" you can change the style of lettering, point size, make it bold or italics, and several other features relating to the appearance of the lettering.

If you point at the value axis and double click the left mouse button, you can change the appearance of that axis in several ways. Besides changing the font of the numbers on the axis, you can also choose "Scale" from the menus presented and change the minimum, maximum, and major or minor units represented on that axis. This can change the look of a chart tremendously.

Another way to format a chart is to point with the mouse at the item you wish to change, click once with the left mouse button to select the item, then click once with the right mouse button. A menu box will appear that offers choices as to what you wish to do next. Among the alternatives will be a formatting choice. By clicking on that choice, the same dialog box will appear that was presented by double clicking the left mouse button as discussed earlier.

Enhancing The Chart With Arrows And Text

Up to this point, all of our formatting changes have involved changing items that were already in the chart. These items are called "attached text" because the program attaches them to the chart where it wants them to appear. The title always appears at the top of the chart. The axes titles always appear next to and below the appropriate axis. There is no choice as to where these items will be placed by the program. But Excel also allows the use of "unattached text." This is text that is placed exactly where you want it to appear.

To add unattached text to an embedded chart, double click on the chart to make it active and simply type the piece of text you wish to add. The text will appear in the formula bar as you type it. Press the Enter key and the program will automatically place that text in approximately the middle of the chart. Point at the text with the mouse, hold down the left mouse button and drag the text to where you want it placed. Release the mouse button and the text is deposited. Unattached text can be formatted, just as attached text can be. To add unattached text to a chart that is a separate window, you do not need to double click on the chart, since it is the only occupant of the window it does not need to be selected. Follow the other steps as you would for an embedded chart.

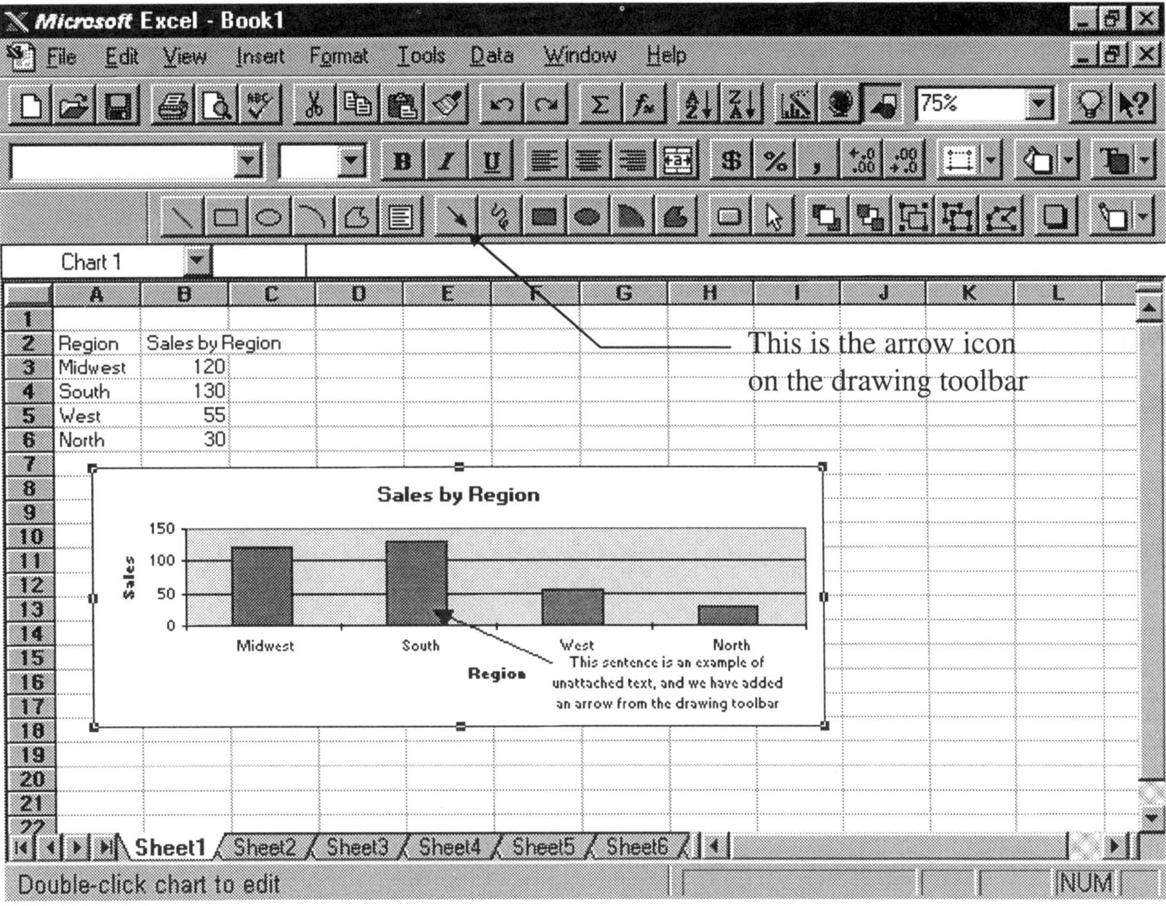

Arrows can also be added to a chart for emphasis. To add an arrow, choose View Toolbars from the menus and then click on the box next to the word "Drawing" in the list of available toolbars and click on "OK." This will add another toolbar to your screen that is not normally in view. Click with the left mouse button on the arrow icon, then move the mouse to the place where you want the arrow to begin (the non-pointed end). Click and hold the left mouse button and drag to form your arrow. It can be as long or short as you wish and can point in any direction on the chart. When the arrow looks the way you want it to look, release the mouse button. An arrow, combined with unattached text, can emphasize a particular value or portion of a chart that you want to make sure your audience does not miss.

PRINTING

When an Excel worksheet is displayed on the computer screen, it is a "soft copy" of the work, but sometimes you need a copy that you can take with you to a meeting or one on which you can make written notes. Printing allows you to obtain a "hard copy" of your worksheet or chart. If you are printing a small worksheet, choose File Print from the menus and when the dialog box appears on the screen, click on the OK button. By default, Excel will print one copy of the entire worksheet.

Printing A Selection

There are times, however, when just a portion of a spreadsheet needs to be printed. For example, some professors keep track of students' grades by using a spreadsheet. When the grades are posted, the spreadsheet can be printed omitting the column with the students' names for privacy reasons. In this case, we would want to print only part of the spreadsheet, not the whole thing. To do this, start by highlighting the section of the spreadsheet you wish to print, then choose File Print from the menus. A dialog box will appear. In the center left part of the box will be a section titled "Print What" and the first option is "Selection." By choosing this option, the program will print only that part of the spreadsheet that you have highlighted. From this point, you can just click on the OK button, or you can first choose how many copies of the document you want printed.

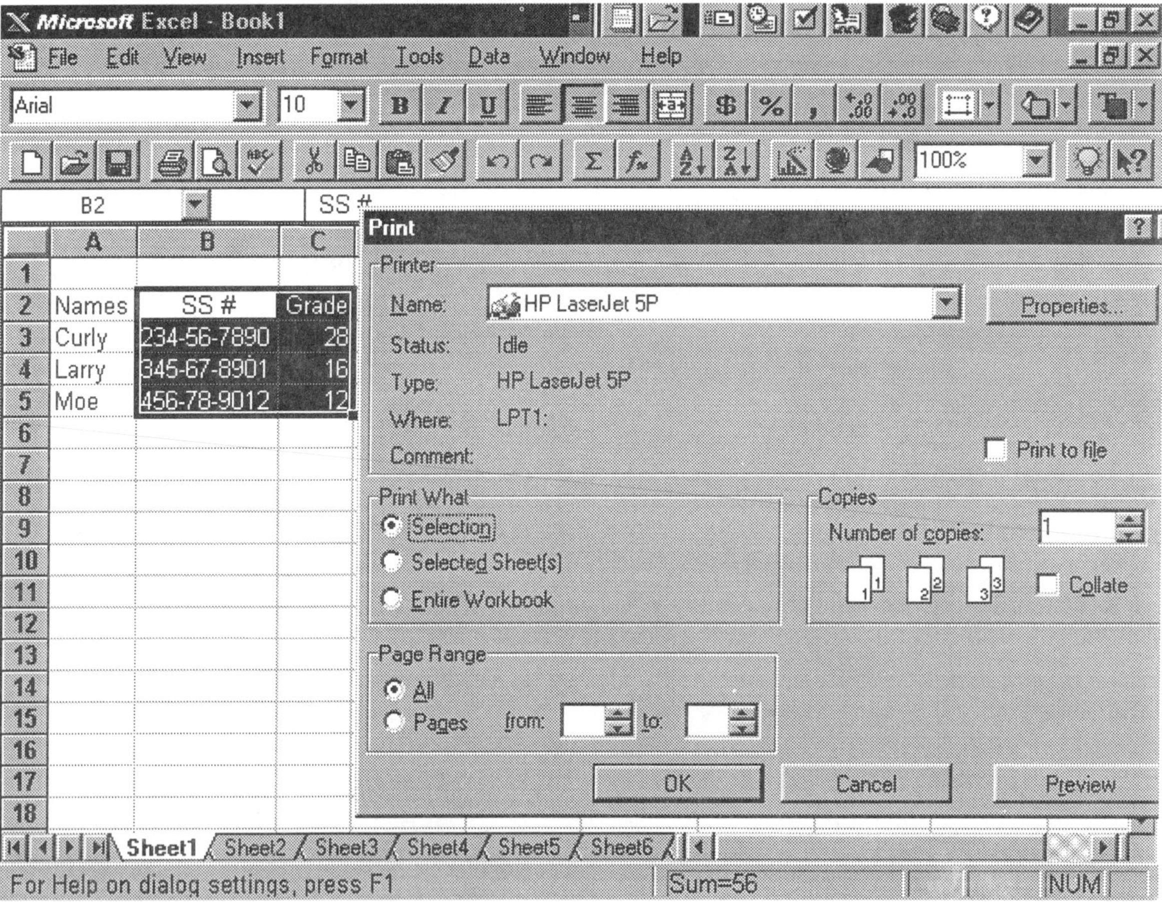

Print Orientation

There are also some other choices we can make when we print a spreadsheet. Choose File Page Setup from the menus, then choose Page from the selections and a dialog box will appear that offers some alternatives as to how the spreadsheet will look when it is printed. First, you have a choice of printing in Portrait or Landscape orientation. Portrait means your spreadsheet will print normally, 8 ½ inches wide by 11 inches long. Landscape turns your spreadsheet sideways for printing so that the paper is 11 inches wide and 8 ½ inches tall. Some spreadsheets look better in one orientation rather than the other.

Fitting The Spreadsheet To A Single Page

Another option available in this dialog box is the scaling of the printout. If the spreadsheet is larger than one page, but you really want it to print all on one page, choose the "Fit to" option under Scaling. By default, Excel will fill in the number of pages as "Fit to 1 page wide by 1 page tall." The program will do everything in its power to reduce the size of the spreadsheet so that it will fit on one page for printing.

What You See Is What You Get (WYSIWYG)

If you are not confident that your spreadsheet will print the way you want, it is a good idea to view the spreadsheet before you print, just to make sure you do not waste paper printing something that does not look right. To view the spreadsheet just as it will print, choose File Print Preview from the menus. Your spreadsheet will appear exactly as it will print. If it is too small to read, click on the "Zoom" option. Notice at this point the mouse pointer becomes an icon of a magnifying glass as you inspect your work. If you are happy with what you see, choose "Print." If you wish to make changes before you print, choose "Close" and the program returns you to the spreadsheet in normal view. An option such as Print Preview which allows you to view exactly what will print is called WYSIWYG (wiz'-ee-wig), an acronym for "What You See Is What You Get." This is available in most programs now, including spreadsheets as well as word processing programs. The purpose is to save time and paper by avoiding wasted printouts.

Printing Charts

To print a chart that has been created as a separate window, simply bring the chart up on your screen and follow the normal procedures for printing. However, if you created your chart on top of the spreadsheet and you want to print it on a separate page, begin by double clicking on the chart to put it into the edit mode. Choose File Print from the menus and continue as you normally would print, selecting the orientation, number of copies, and anything else you wish to choose.

If you want to print the chart on the same page as the worksheet, select the range you wish to print, including both the spreadsheet and the chart in that range. Choose File Print from the menus and continue as usual in printing your work.

OPENING EXISTING FILES

Once you have created and saved a file, you may wish to open it again sometime in the future. To open an existing file, choose File Open from the menus and a dialog box will appear from which you may select the file you wish to open.

QUITTING EXCEL

There are several ways to exit the Excel program. The quickest way is to click one time with the left mouse button on the "X" at the far right side of the title bar. Another way to close the program is to double click the left mouse button on the application control button, located at the far left end of the title bar. You can also close Excel by choosing File Exit from the menus. Notice that if you attempt to close the Excel program without saving your work,

Excel will display a dialog box on the screen that asks if you wish to save the changes that have been made in your work.

COMPREHENSIVE EXAMPLE

To help you apply the concepts and tools discussed so far we next provide a comprehensive example using Excel to solve a finance problem. The problem is given below and a step by step solution follows. This example has been selected because it allows us to demonstrate a large number of methods that may be helpful to you in other applications.

Example: Soft drink production expansion

A firm is considering expanding its line of soft drinks as a result of capturing market share. The new production line will cost $250,000 plus $100,000 for a new building and installation. Net working capital is expected to increase by $50,000. The new line will be depreciated over its expected 7 year life using straight line depreciation. Revenues generated by the new line are expected to be $20,000 the first year and are expected to increase at a rate of $5,000 per year thereafter. Operating costs are expected to be $10,000 in the first year and are expected to increase at a rate of $1,500 per year thereafter. After 7 years the project will have a salvage value of $10,000. The firm has a cost of capital of 12% and a tax rate of 40%. What are the net initial investment and the annual cash flows associated with the project? Compute the net present value of the cash flows.

Solution:

Problems of this nature where multiple years of cash flows must be manipulated are most easily solved using a spreadsheet program. Once the first year cash flows are entered we will be able to compute the rest of the annual cash flows by using formulas and copy commands. Let us begin by computing the initial investment.

Step 1: The initial investment

The initial investment is the sum of the purchase price, installation, shipping and working capital. We will place this on the same worksheet as the annual cash flows since the total initial investment must be subtracted from the present value of the annual cash flows to prepare a net present value profile. The figures given in the problem are in rows 2-5 and the sum function is used to compute the net investment in row 6.

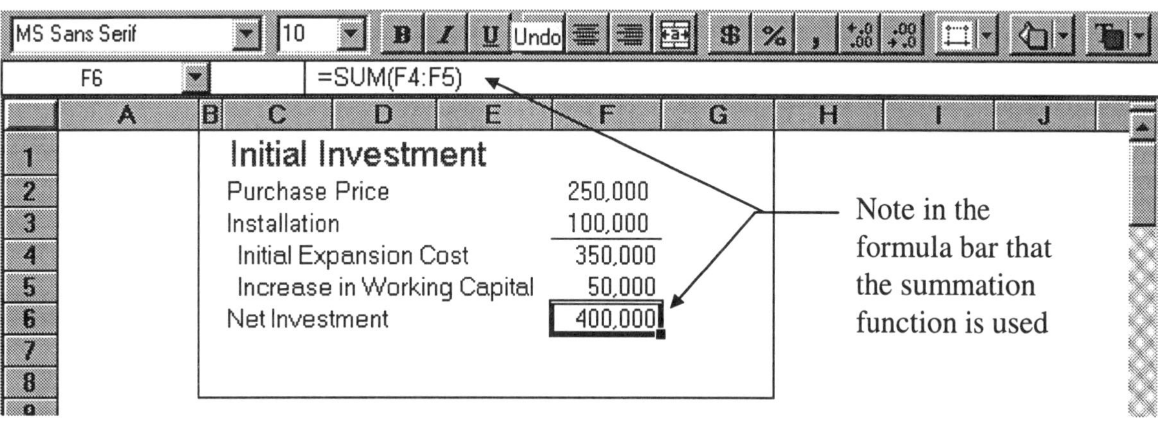

Step 2: The worksheet titles

The next step is to lay out the cash flow section of the worksheet by typing in the row and column headings. This is done below.

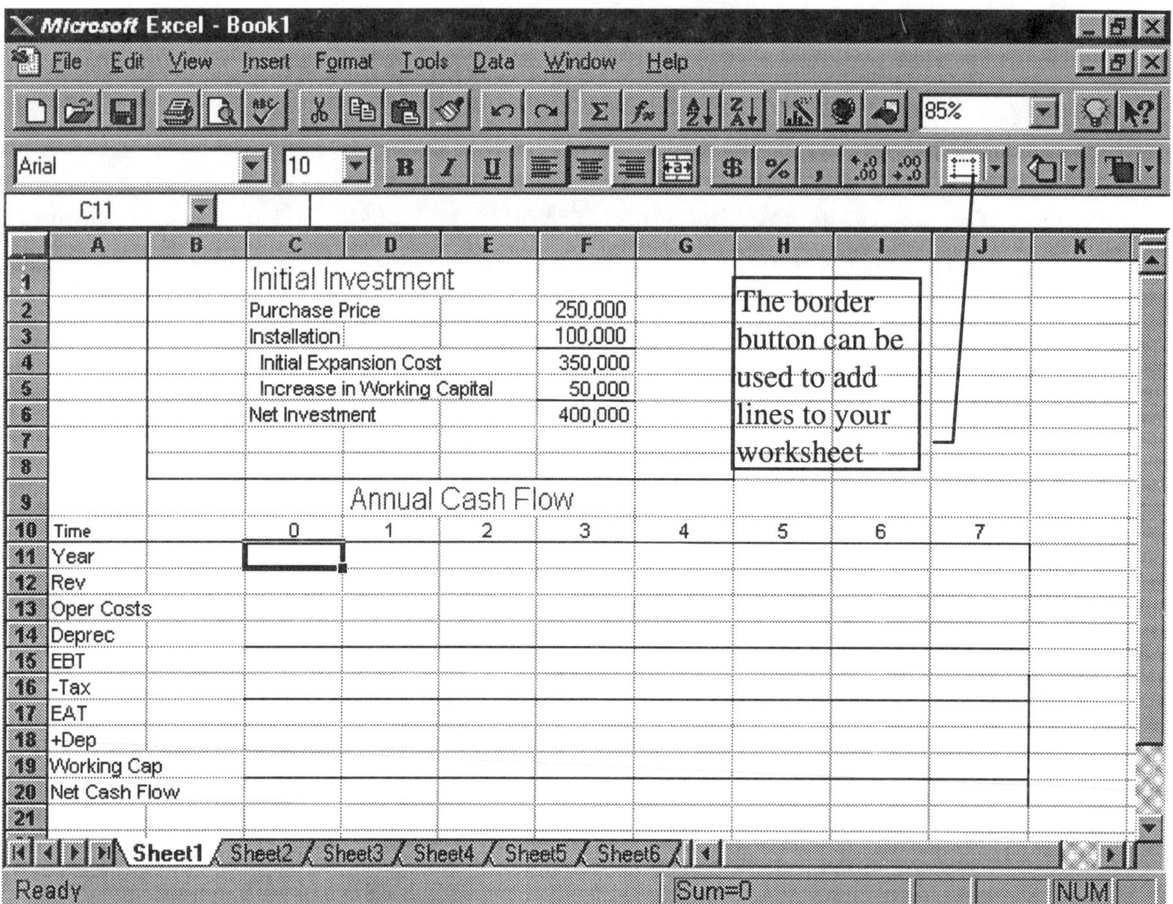

A year 0 is included to represent the present. Lines are added to the spreadsheet to make it easier to read. You could also choose to color the titles if the final version will be printed on a color printer.

Step 3: Entering the first year's cash flows

The first year's cash flows are entered into column D. Use formulas wherever possible so that most of the work will be done for you when you copy column D into the other columns. For example, earnings before tax (EBT) is highlighted so that you can see the formula. You may also choose to add $ signs and parentheses to your table to make it look more professional and easier to read.

Note that the annual depreciation is the formula ($F$6-10,000 / 7). It takes the total initial cost from cell F6, subtracts the salvage value and divides by 7 to compute the annual straight line depreciation. The dollar signs keep the reference absolute so that when the formula is copied the reference to cell F6 does not change. This way, if your estimate of the initial costs change, only one cell on the spreadsheet will have to be changed. The rest will automatically re-compute.

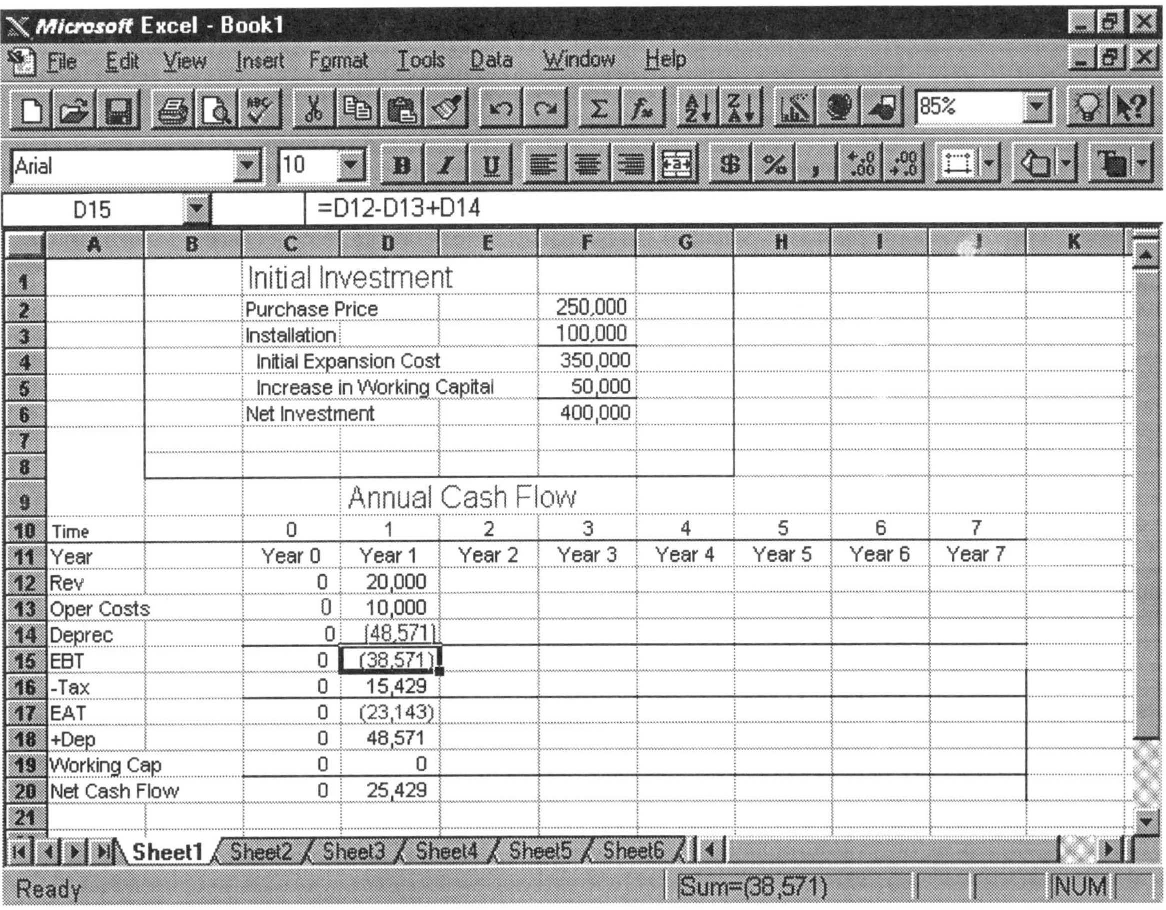

Initial Investment

Purchase Price	250,000
Installation	100,000
Initial Expansion Cost	350,000
Increase in Working Capital	50,000
Net Investment	400,000

Annual Cash Flow

Time	0	1	2	3	4	5	6	7
Year	Year 0	Year 1	Year 2	Year 3	Year 4	Year 5	Year 6	Year 7
Rev	0	20,000						
Oper Costs	0	10,000						
Deprec	0	(48,571)						
EBT	0	(38,571)						
-Tax	0	15,429						
EAT	0	(23,143)						
+Dep	0	48,571						
Working Cap	0	0						
Net Cash Flow	0	25,429						

Step 4: Year 2 formulas

In year 2, revenues are expected to rise by $5,000 and operating cost by $1,500. We will impute this information as formulas. For example, year 2 revenues will be entered as (=D12+5000). Similarly operating costs are entered as (=D13+1500). Cells 14-19 can just be copied from column D to column E.

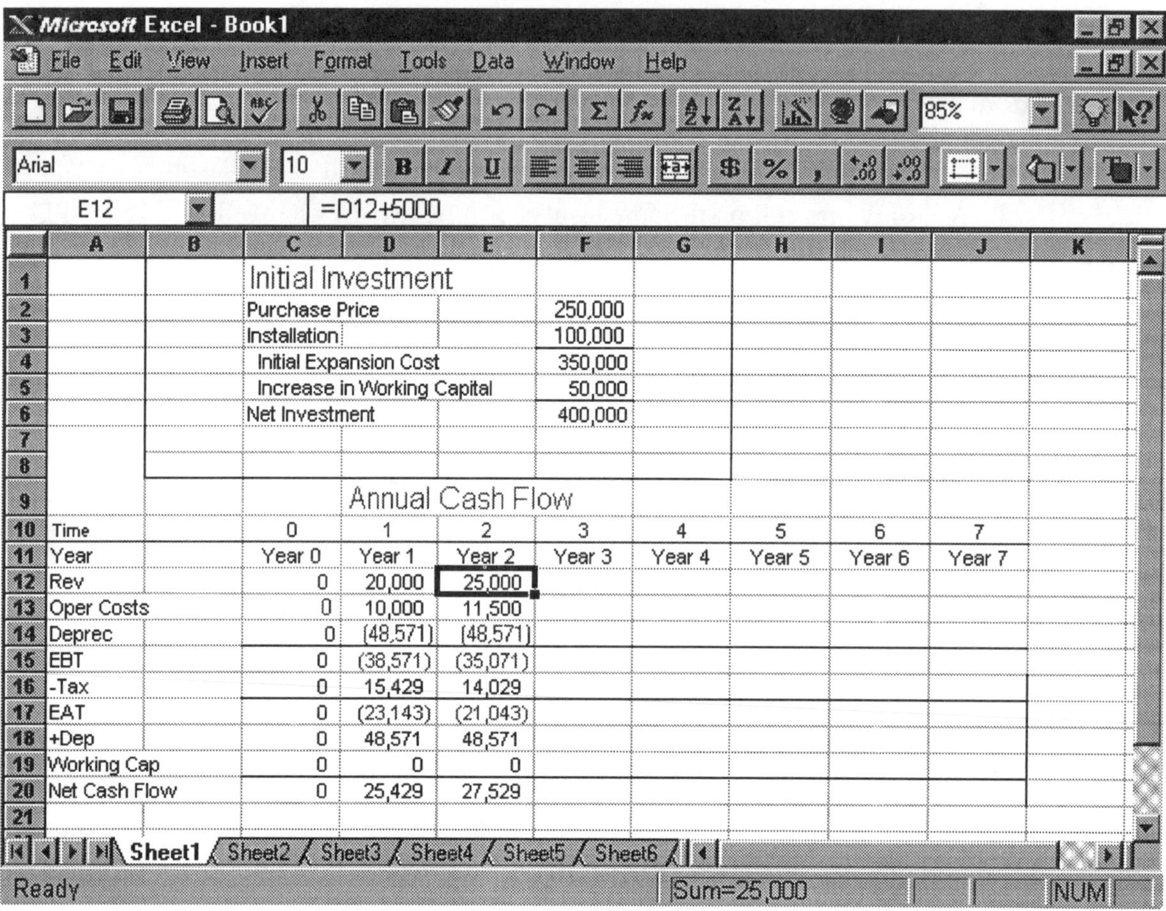

E12 =D12+5000

	A	B	C	D	E	F	G	H	I	J
1			Initial Investment							
2			Purchase Price			250,000				
3			Installation			100,000				
4			Initial Expansion Cost			350,000				
5			Increase in Working Capital			50,000				
6			Net Investment			400,000				
7										
8										
9				Annual Cash Flow						
10	Time		0	1	2	3	4	5	6	7
11	Year		Year 0	Year 1	Year 2	Year 3	Year 4	Year 5	Year 6	Year 7
12	Rev		0	20,000	25,000					
13	Oper Costs		0	10,000	11,500					
14	Deprec		0	(48,571)	(48,571)					
15	EBT		0	(38,571)	(35,071)					
16	-Tax		0	15,429	14,029					
17	EAT		0	(23,143)	(21,043)					
18	+Dep		0	48,571	48,571					
19	Working Cap		0	0	0					
20	Net Cash Flow		0	25,429	27,529					

As soon as you copied cells D14-D20 to cells E14-E20, all of the formulas automatically recalculated. The new net cash flow in cell E20 reflects the additional revenues and operating costs.

Step 5: Copying to the rest of the spreadsheet

This next step is where we really see the power of electronic spreadsheets. It took a little longer to prepare year 1 and 2 cash flows than if we had just entered the figures because we wanted to use formulas. This extra effort pays off now because we can simply copy year two cash flow over into years 3-7. All of the formulas update the cells and the annual cash flows are correctly computed. We copy the year two cells by highlighting the range of cells E12-E20, and dragging the small square box at the lower right side across the columns we wish to fill. As soon as we release the mouse button the cells are updated.

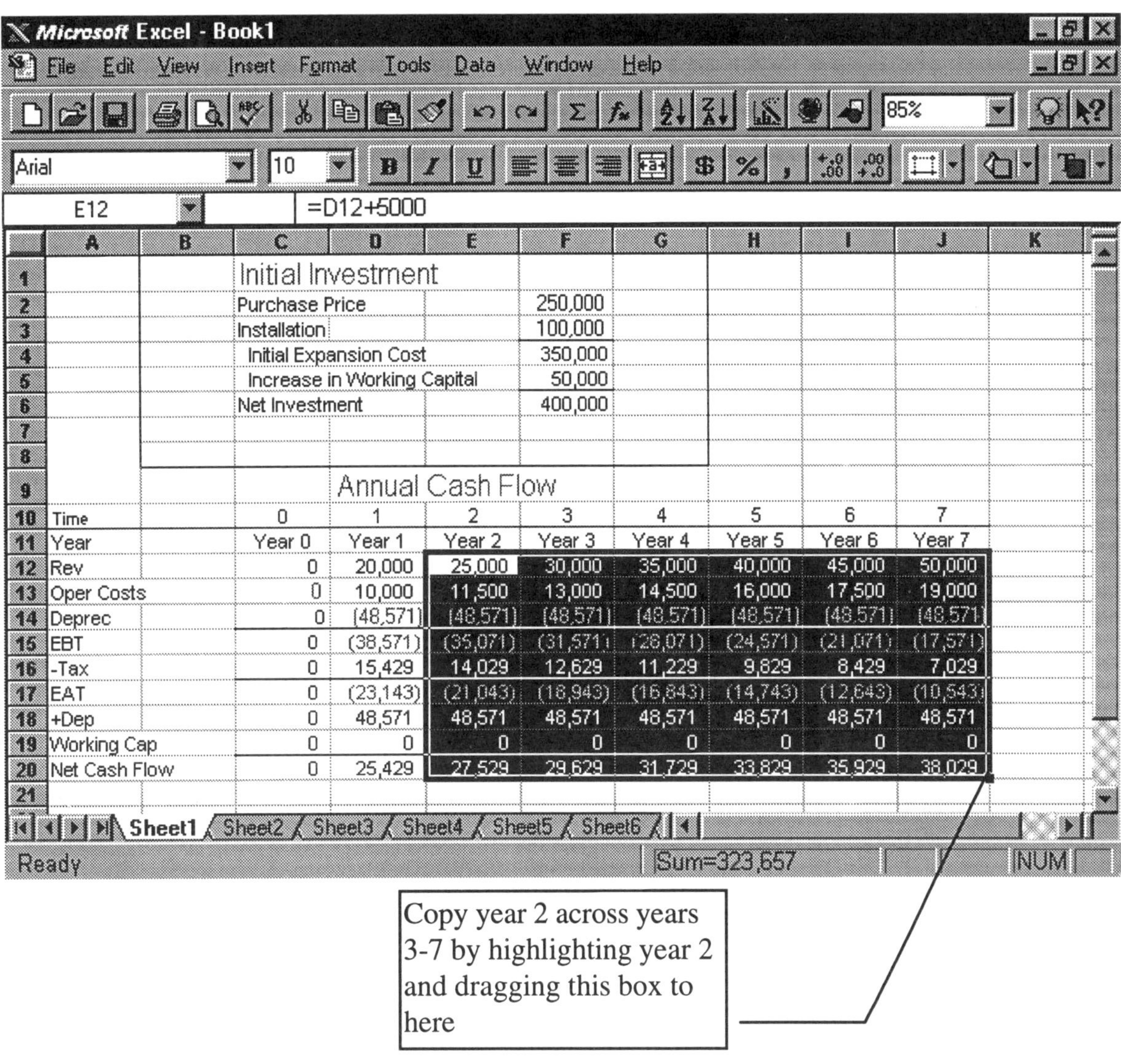

Initial Investment

Purchase Price	250,000
Installation	100,000
Initial Expansion Cost	350,000
Increase in Working Capital	50,000
Net Investment	400,000

Annual Cash Flow

Time	0	1	2	3	4	5	6	7
Year	Year 0	Year 1	Year 2	Year 3	Year 4	Year 5	Year 6	Year 7
Rev	0	20,000	25,000	30,000	35,000	40,000	45,000	50,000
Oper Costs	0	10,000	11,500	13,000	14,500	16,000	17,500	19,000
Deprec	0	(48,571)	(48,571)	(48,571)	(48,571)	(48,571)	(48,571)	(48,571)
EBT	0	(38,571)	(35,071)	(31,571)	(28,071)	(24,571)	(21,071)	(17,571)
-Tax	0	15,429	14,029	12,629	11,229	9,829	8,429	7,029
EAT	0	(23,143)	(21,043)	(18,943)	(16,843)	(14,743)	(12,643)	(10,543)
+Dep	0	48,571	48,571	48,571	48,571	48,571	48,571	48,571
Working Cap	0	0	0	0	0	0	0	0
Net Cash Flow	0	25,429	27,529	29,629	31,729	33,829	35,929	38,029

Step 6: Adding salvage and working capital

When we prepared row titles for the worksheet we remembered that in the final year we would need to account for recapturing working capital. Since this is 0 for the years 1-6, we will have to update year 7 to reflect this unique year 7 entry.

In this step we will also add a new line to the spreadsheet to allow for the salvage value of the soft drink equipment. We left this off the original template to demonstrate another powerful feature of electronic spreadsheets. If we note an error or wish to add a row or column, it is easy and quick to make adjustments.

To add a row to the spreadsheet, highlight the row just below where you want the row to be placed. If you want to add more than one row, highlight as many as you wish to add. It can be difficult to remember whether you need to highlight the row just above or just below the insertion point. Just remember that if you wanted to add a row to the very top of the spreadsheet it would be impossible to highlight above. It is a good idea to manually check a column or two to verify that the spreadsheet is working as you expect. Note the error we created in the box at the bottom of this page.

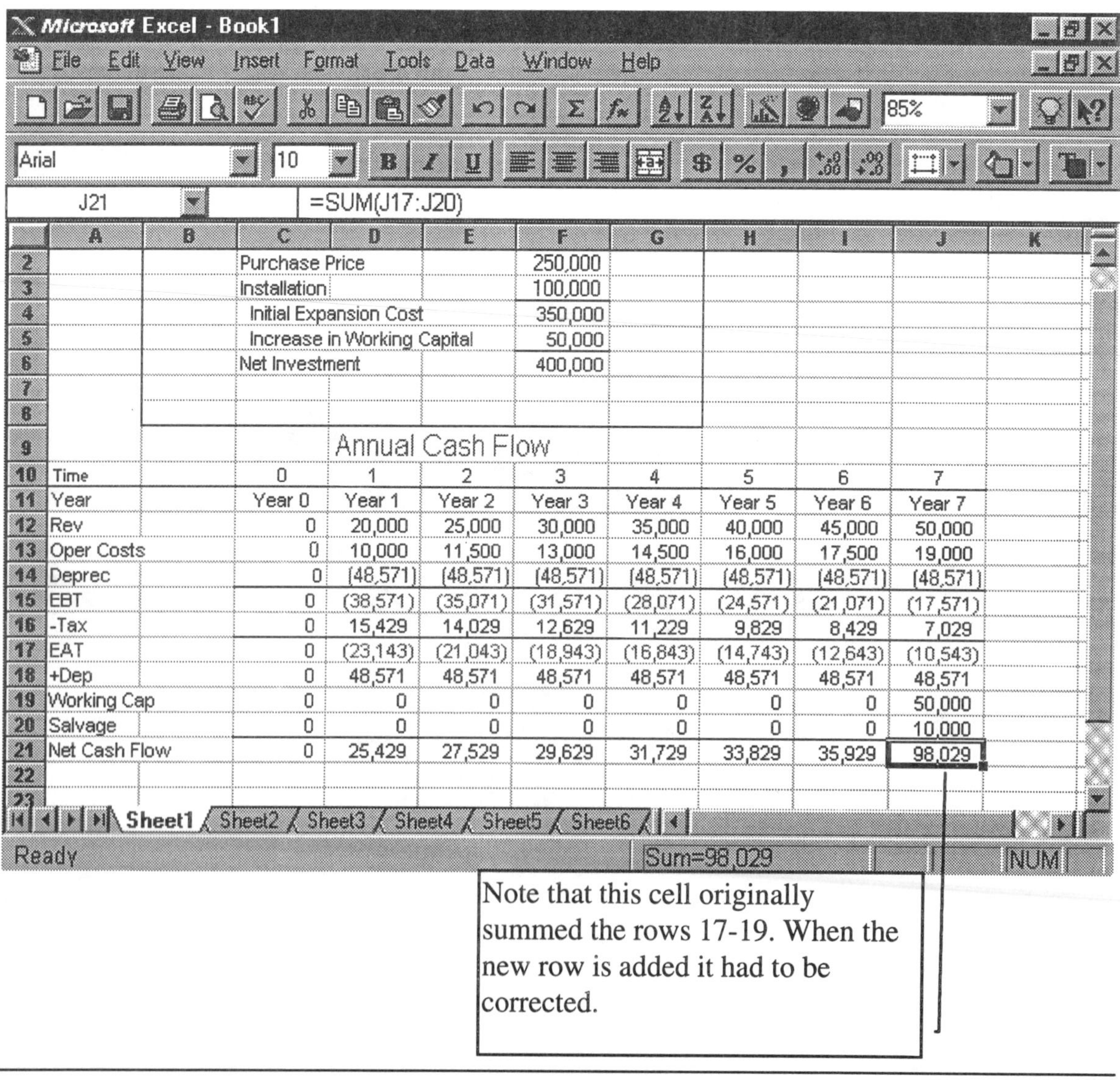

Microsoft Excel - Book1

J21 =SUM(J17:J20)

	A	B	C	D	E	F	G	H	I	J
2			Purchase Price			250,000				
3			Installation			100,000				
4			Initial Expansion Cost			350,000				
5			Increase in Working Capital			50,000				
6			Net Investment			400,000				
7										
8										
9				Annual Cash Flow						
10	Time		0	1	2	3	4	5	6	7
11	Year		Year 0	Year 1	Year 2	Year 3	Year 4	Year 5	Year 6	Year 7
12	Rev		0	20,000	25,000	30,000	35,000	40,000	45,000	50,000
13	Oper Costs		0	10,000	11,500	13,000	14,500	16,000	17,500	19,000
14	Deprec		0	(48,571)	(48,571)	(48,571)	(48,571)	(48,571)	(48,571)	(48,571)
15	EBT		0	(38,571)	(35,071)	(31,571)	(28,071)	(24,571)	(21,071)	(17,571)
16	-Tax		0	15,429	14,029	12,629	11,229	9,829	8,429	7,029
17	EAT		0	(23,143)	(21,043)	(18,943)	(16,843)	(14,743)	(12,643)	(10,543)
18	+Dep		0	48,571	48,571	48,571	48,571	48,571	48,571	48,571
19	Working Cap		0	0	0	0	0	0	0	50,000
20	Salvage		0	0	0	0	0	0	0	10,000
21	Net Cash Flow		0	25,429	27,529	29,629	31,729	33,829	35,929	98,029

Sheet1 Sheet2 Sheet3 Sheet4 Sheet5 Sheet6

Ready Sum=98,029 NUM

Note that this cell originally summed the rows 17-19. When the new row is added it had to be corrected.

Step 7: Computing the net present value

We are now ready to compute the net present value of the cash flows. We can find out how the present value function must be formatted by using the help button or by using the Function Wizard. The current example was prepared by choosing help index from the help menu, typing in "functions" and choosing the function index option. We then selected financial functions and PV to determine how to format the function command. This command is formatted as: PV(rate, nper, pmt, fv, type). Each of these factors is described in the help text. Rate is the discount rate (in whole number percentage), nper is the number of periods, fv is the future value, pmt is the payment if the cash flow is an annuity and type is equal to 0 if the payment is received at the end of the period, and 1 if at the beginning.

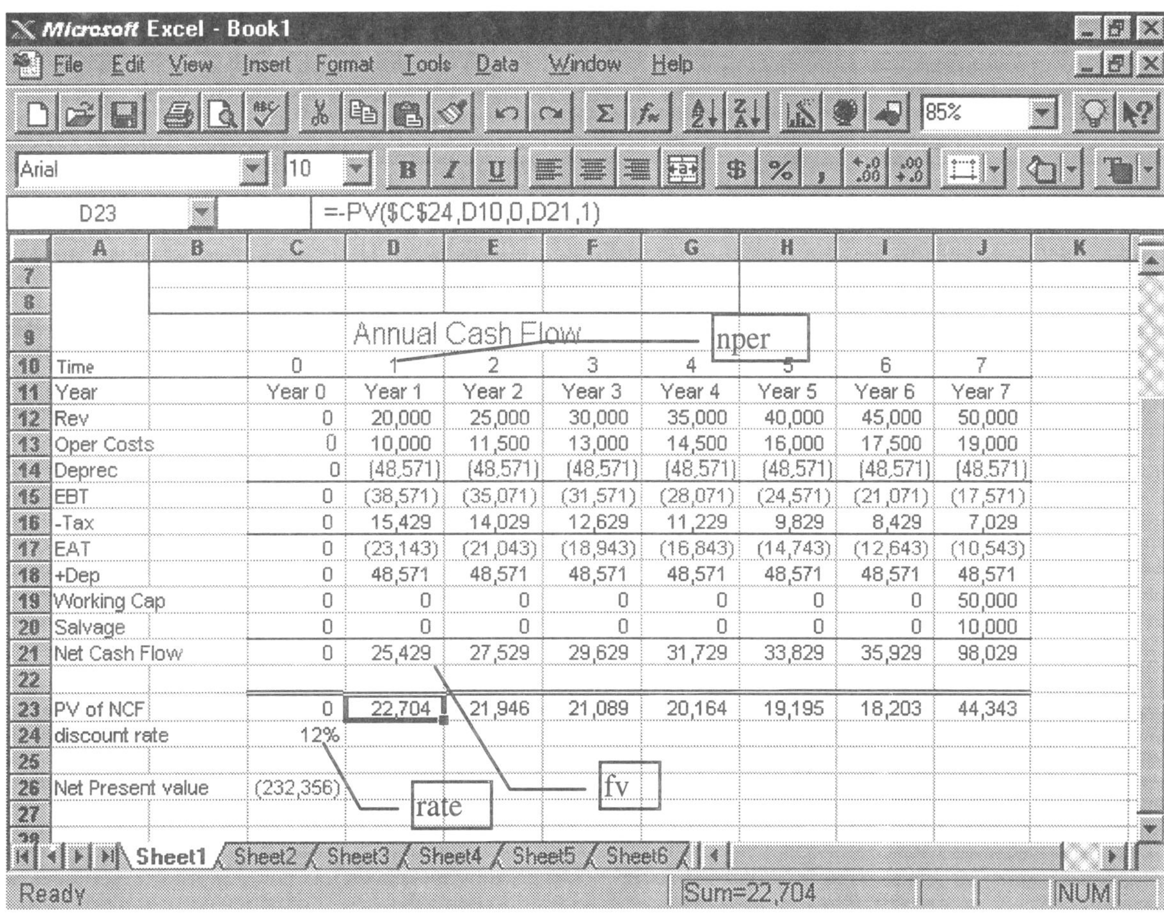

Microsoft Excel - Book1

D23 =-PV($C$24,D10,0,D21,1)

	A	C	D	E	F	G	H	I	J
9			Annual Cash Flow						
10	Time	0	1	2	3	4	5	6	7
11	Year	Year 0	Year 1	Year 2	Year 3	Year 4	Year 5	Year 6	Year 7
12	Rev	0	20,000	25,000	30,000	35,000	40,000	45,000	50,000
13	Oper Costs	0	10,000	11,500	13,000	14,500	16,000	17,500	19,000
14	Deprec	0	(48,571)	(48,571)	(48,571)	(48,571)	(48,571)	(48,571)	(48,571)
15	EBT	0	(38,571)	(35,071)	(31,571)	(28,071)	(24,571)	(21,071)	(17,571)
16	-Tax	0	15,429	14,029	12,629	11,229	9,829	8,429	7,029
17	EAT	0	(23,143)	(21,043)	(18,943)	(16,843)	(14,743)	(12,643)	(10,543)
18	+Dep	0	48,571	48,571	48,571	48,571	48,571	48,571	48,571
19	Working Cap	0	0	0	0	0	0	0	50,000
20	Salvage	0	0	0	0	0	0	0	10,000
21	Net Cash Flow	0	25,429	27,529	29,629	31,729	33,829	35,929	98,029
22									
23	PV of NCF	0	22,704	21,946	21,089	20,164	19,195	18,203	44,343
24	discount rate	12%							
25									
26	Net Present value	(232,356)							

Notice how the PV function is set up with cell references so that it can be copied across the years. The reference to the discount rate was made absolute by using dollar signs ($).

Step 8: Graphing the annual cash flows

We can easily graph the annual cash flows using the Chart Wizard.

	A	B	C	D	E	F	G	H	I	J	K
10	Time		0	1	2	3	4	5	6	7	
11	Year		Year 0	Year 1	Year 2	Year 3	Year 4	Year 5	Year 6	Year 7	
12	Rev		0	20,000	25,000	30,000	35,000	40,000	45,000	50,000	
13	Oper Costs		0	10,000	11,500	13,000	14,500	16,000	17,500	19,000	
14	Deprec		0	(48,571)	(48,571)	(48,571)	(48,571)	(48,571)	(48,571)	(48,571)	
15	EBT		0	(38,571)	(35,071)	(31,571)	(28,071)	(24,571)	(21,071)	(17,571)	
16	-Tax		0								
17	EAT		0								
18	+Dep		0								
19	Working Cap		0								
20	Salvage		0								
21	Net Cash Flow		0								
22											
23	PV of NCF		0								
24	discount rate		12%								
25											
26	Net Present value		(232,356)								
27											

ChartWizard - Step 1 of 5

If the selected cells do not contain the data you wish to chart, select a new range now.

Include the cells containing row and column labels if you want those labels to appear on the chart.

Range: =$D$10:$J$10,$D$21:$J$21

Cancel | < Back | Next > | Finish

We began by selecting cells D11-J11 and D21-J21. This is done by selecting the one range of cells and, while holding the control key down, selecting the second range of cells. Note that the chart wizard will automatically add dollar signs to the range selection signifying that this is an absolute reference. With the ranges selected choose **Insert Chart**. Choose to have the chart on the current worksheet. Your pointer will change to a chart icon. Put this where you want the graph to be on your spreadsheet and press enter. The above screen will be displayed.

Choose Next if the cell reference is correct and select the chart style you desire. We will construct a 3-D column chart. Choose next.

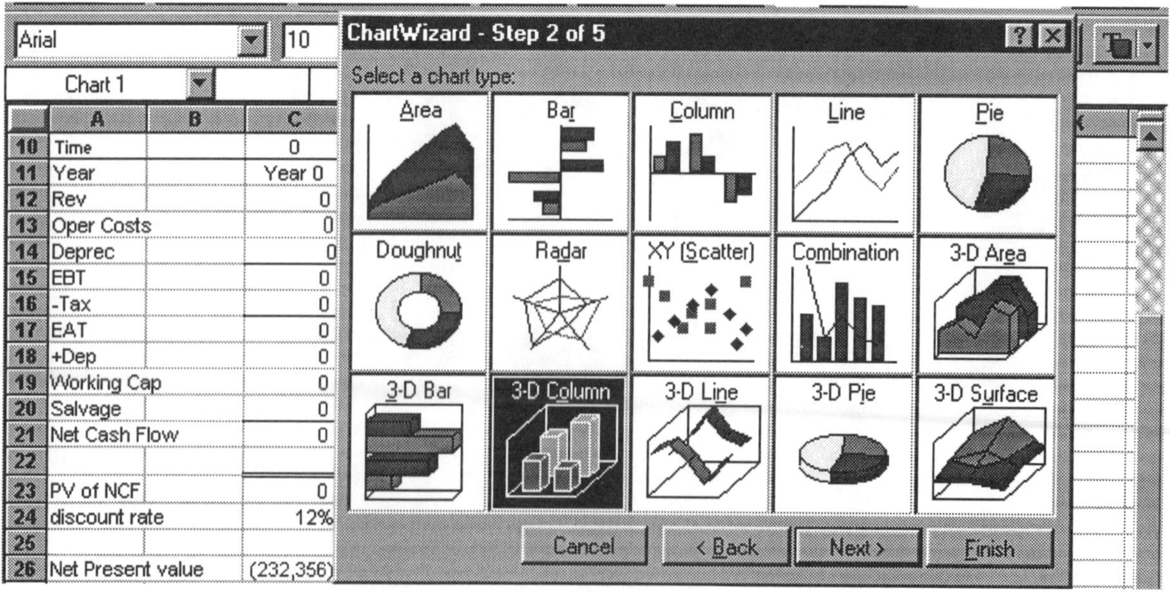

Select Next again to choose the type of column chart you want. You will then be given the following screen to use to organize your data by rows or columns and to tell Excel if the headings are in the 1st row or column. You can play with this screen to find the options that work best for your data.

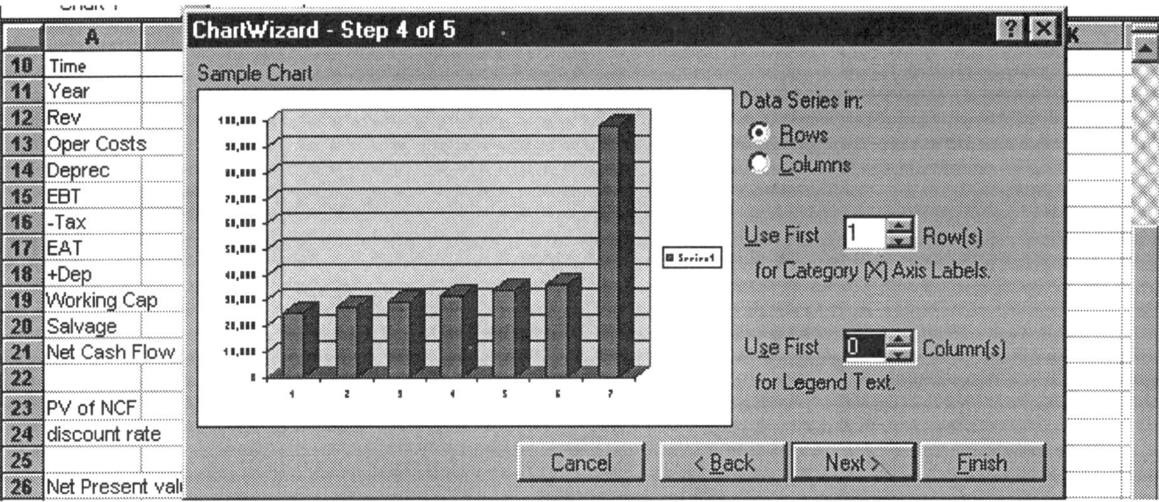

At this point you can either choose Finish and the chart will be placed on your spreadsheet or you can choose Next and have the opportunity to add a chart title and to label the axes. The following is our completed spreadsheet project.

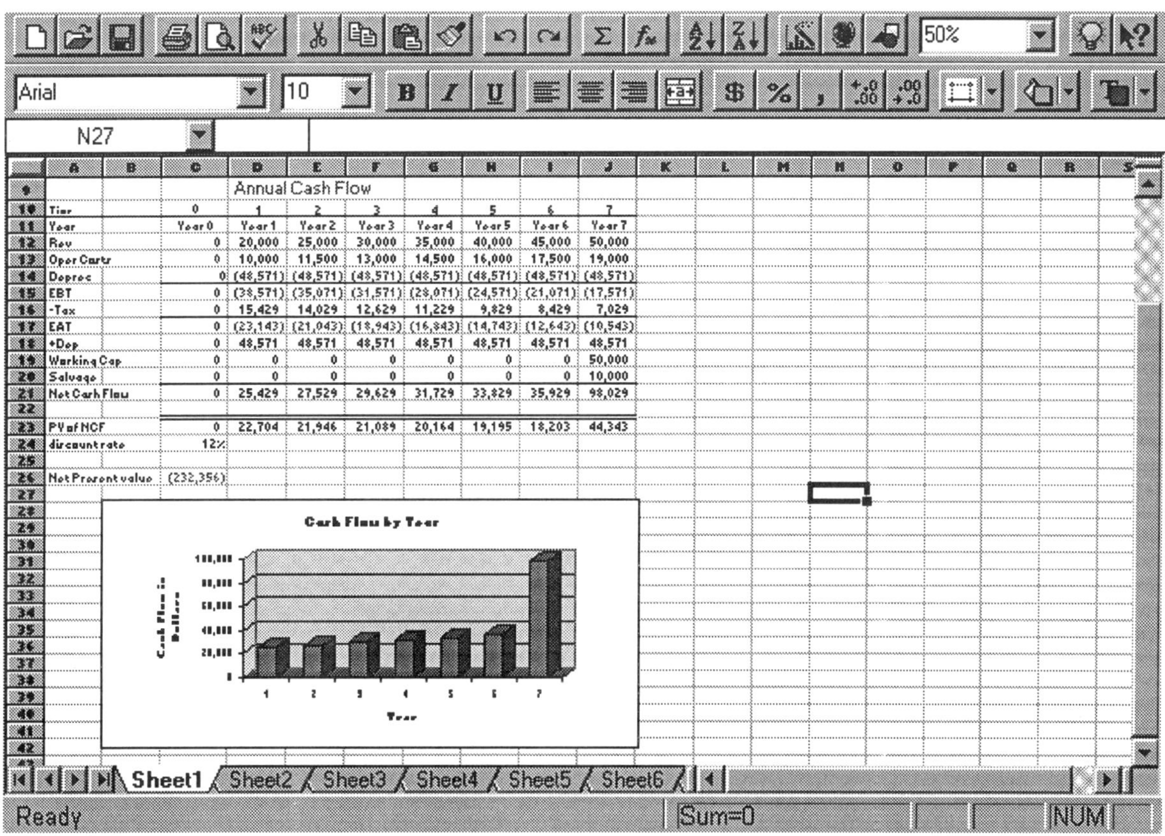

Annual Cash Flow

Time	0	1	2	3	4	5	6	7
Year	Year 0	Year 1	Year 2	Year 3	Year 4	Year 5	Year 6	Year 7
Rev	0	20,000	25,000	30,000	35,000	40,000	45,000	50,000
Oper Costs	0	10,000	11,500	13,000	14,500	16,000	17,500	19,000
Deprec	0	(48,571)	(48,571)	(48,571)	(48,571)	(48,571)	(48,571)	(48,571)
EBT	0	(38,571)	(35,071)	(31,571)	(28,071)	(24,571)	(21,071)	(17,571)
-Tax	0	15,429	14,029	12,629	11,229	9,829	8,429	7,029
EAT	0	(23,143)	(21,043)	(18,943)	(16,843)	(14,743)	(12,643)	(10,543)
+Dep	0	48,571	48,571	48,571	48,571	48,571	48,571	48,571
Working Cap	0	0	0	0	0	0	0	50,000
Salvage	0	0	0	0	0	0	0	10,000
Net Cash Flow	0	25,429	27,529	29,629	31,729	33,829	35,929	98,029
PV of NCF	0	22,704	21,946	21,089	20,164	19,195	18,203	44,343
discount rate	12%							
Net Present value	(232,356)							

Appendix: Lotus 123

Lotus Worksheet Area

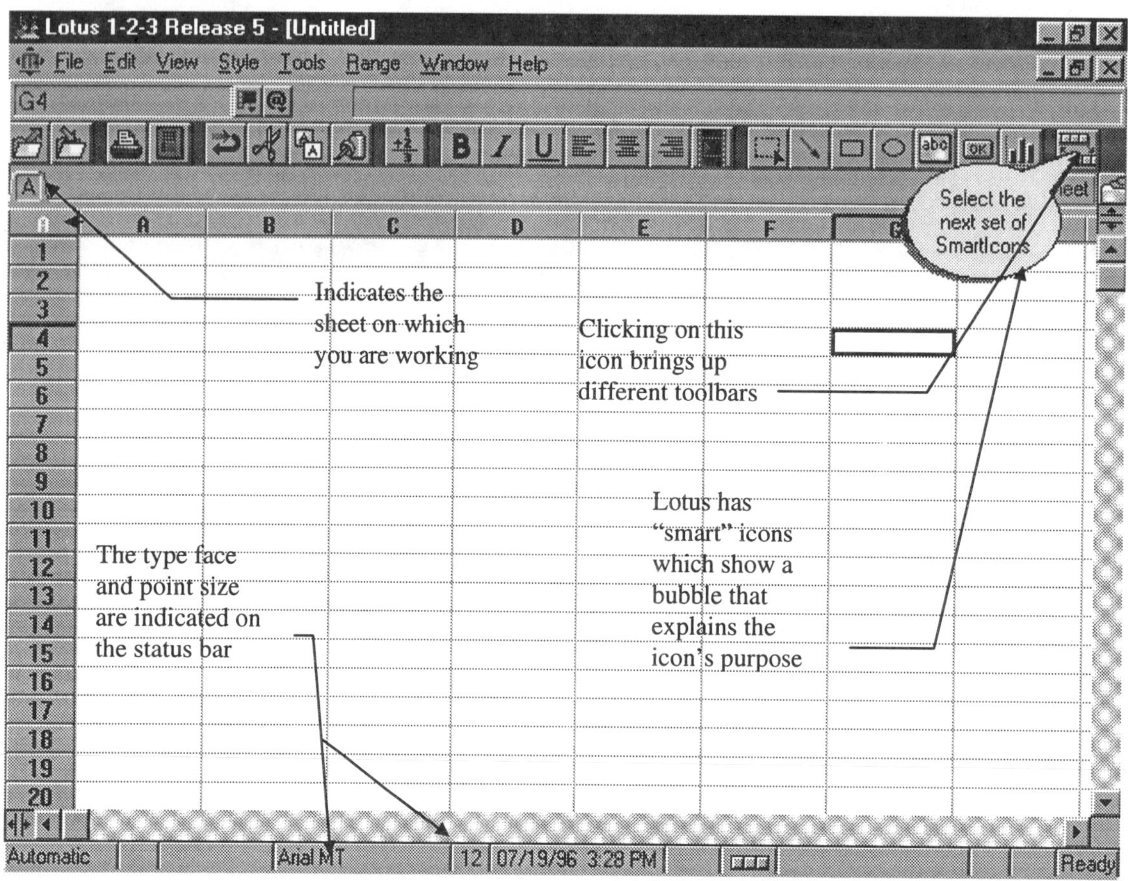

Charts in Lotus

To create a chart using Lotus 123, enter the data into a spreadsheet. Then highlight the data to be included in the chart and choose Tools Chart from the menus. At this point Lotus will look very similar to Excel. A black cross with the icon of a chart attached to it will appear on the spreadsheet. Click the mouse button where you wish the chart to appear and it will be created for you on the spreadsheet.

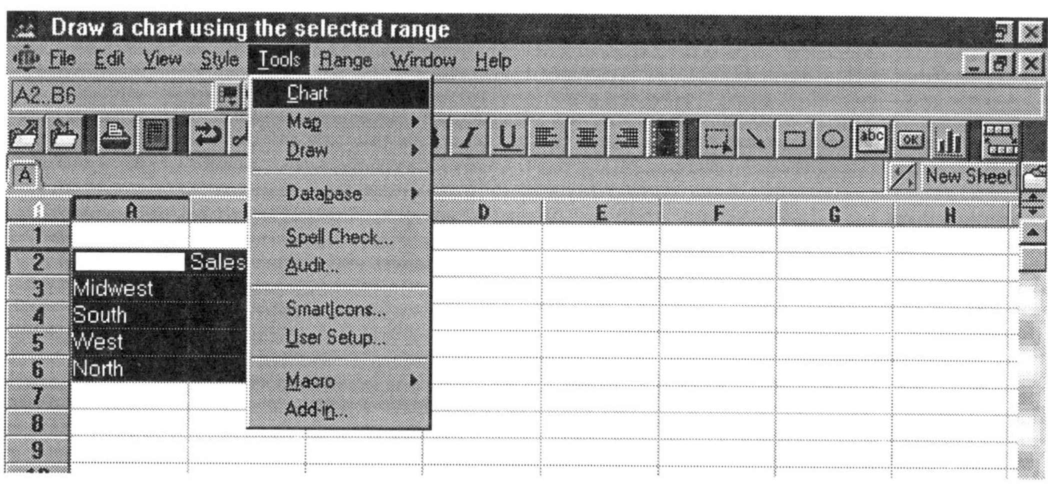

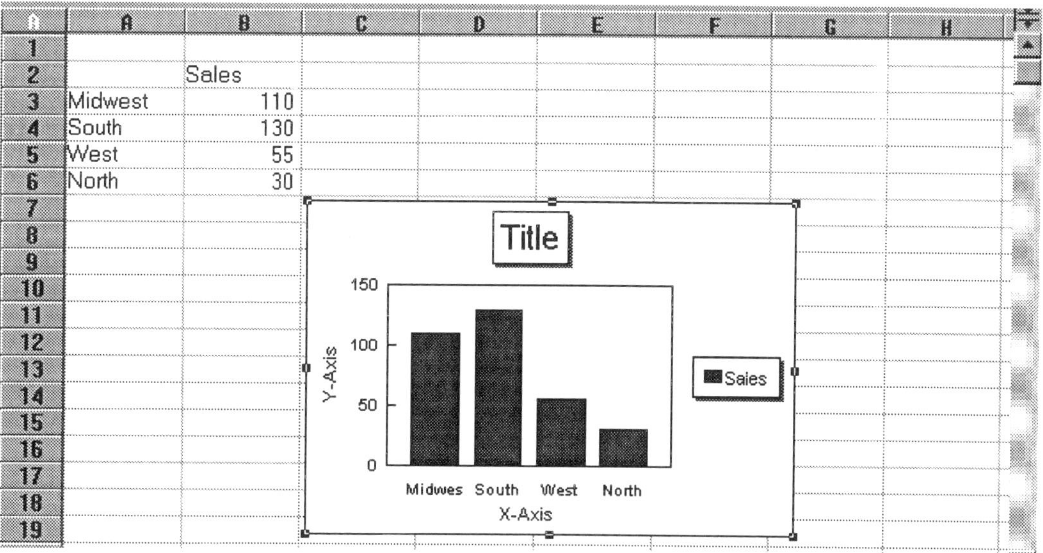

If you wish to create a chart as a separate window in Lotus, it is a little more difficult than it is in Excel. Begin by entering the data into a spreadsheet. Then click on the "New Sheet" button below the toolbar. Go back to the sheet with your data. Highlight the data as you normally would for a chart, choose Tools Chart from the menus, and then go back to the new blank sheet you created. Click the mouse button where you want the chart to appear in the new window and it will be created as a separate sheet.

Adding Titles to the Chart

Lotus creates the chart immediately on your screen with generic titles included. To edit these titles, point at the title you wish to change and double click the left mouse button. A dialog box will appear that allows you to type the title as you wish it to appear. In the example below, the main title at the top of the chart was double clicked upon and the desired title was typed into the dialog box.

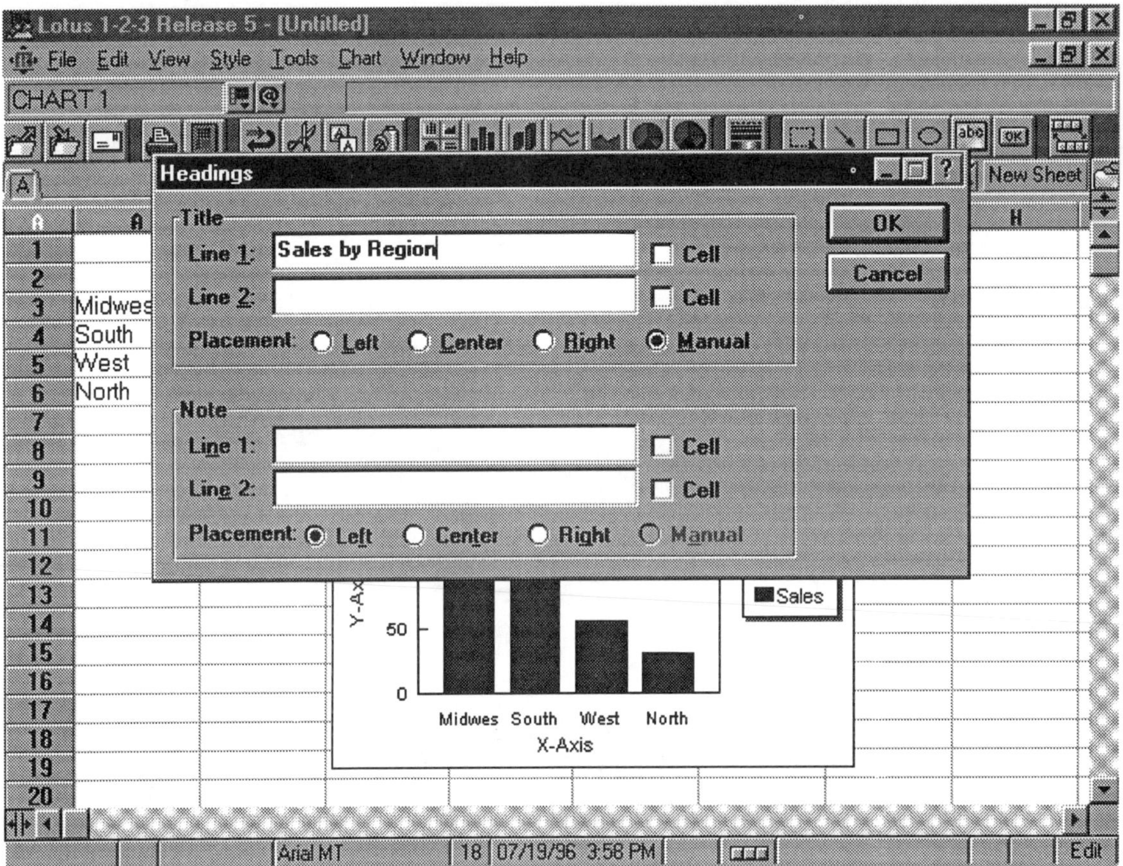

You can also click on the Y axis and X axis labels to rename them. In the example that follows we have completed the chart by labeling the X axis as "Region" and the Y axis as "Sales."

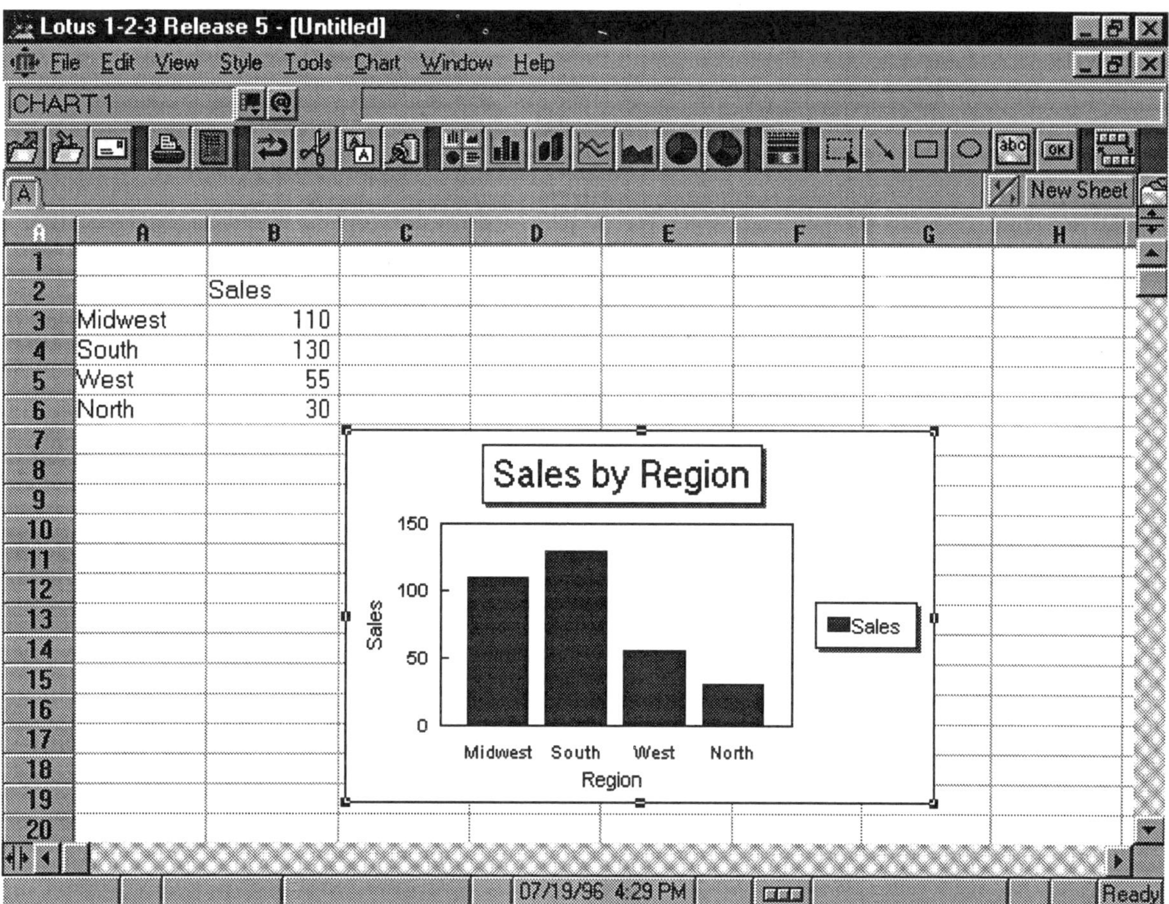
Lotus 1-2-3 Release 5 - [Untitled]
File Edit View Style Tools Chart Window Help
CHART 1
New Sheet
Sales
Midwest 110
South 130
West 55
North 30
Sales by Region
150
100
50
0
Sales
Midwest South West North
Region
Sales
07/19/96 4:29 PM
Ready